And This Gospel of the Kingdom:

Reinterpreting the Gospel in a Post-Colonial Context

Dr. Dana Carson

And This Gospel of the Kingdom

Published in the United States by Dana Carson Kingdom Ministries, Inc.

ISBN: 0-9746616-3-5

Dedication

I want to first dedicate this book to my wife and friend, Rachelle Dianne Carson, my *Baruch*! Knitted to me in the flesh and the spirit, I could not do what I do without her.

To our wonderful children, Dana II and his wife Monet, John Anthony and his daughter Jaide, Angel Naomi, Marielle Alli, and Devon Jarrod, I give my everlasting love and gratitude for their unending sacrifice of me as their father for the betterment of others.

This book is also dedicated…

To my staff who undergirds all of my ministry endeavors.

To my sons and daughter in ministry: Bishop William Kettor; Evangelist Samuel Johnson; Pastors Dr. Charles Moody, Marquet Curl, Andrew Taylor, Tyree Bearden, Lew Williams, Diedre Williams, Mishael Carson, Sechaba Mothiane, Jeremiah Thompsons, Vitalis Nwaiwu, Kennedy Mbuya.

To The R.O.C.K. church family, thank you for sharing me with the world!

And This Gospel of the Kingdom

Contents

And This Gospel of the Kingdom

Foreword

Today, many church-goers and so-called believers say they are committed Christians; however the only time they think about spiritual things is Sunday morning and during crises. Unfortunately today, most Christians lean towards the Laodicean model vs. the Kingdom model for church attendance. The 21st century Christian is totally consumed with his or her own passions, dreams, and desires, and the Laodicean church assuages those desires and encourages them to continue toward their dreams and hopes.

Christ the King and Lord is foreign to the contemporary culture. While the Bible teaches death to one's self and being alive unto God, this is a foreign concept in the mind of many of those who feel they already have a Kingdom reservation in God's heavenly mansion. The contemporary church has made Jesus a cosmic bellhop or a ghetto sugar daddy who is being pimped by the demands of those who will leave Him if He doesn't give them their way. Many contemporary church members have learned how to be Christians without Christ as Lord of their life. Guess you can say they are Sunday morning Christians; however, the Bible doesn't ask us to give God a Sabbath gift and He will be satisfied. The gospel of the Kingdom or the dominion/reign of God was the message that Christ and His disciples proclaimed. The Bible is very clear that the Newer Testament message of Christ and the early church was the gospel of the Kingdom.

In order for one to enter the Kingdom, the Bible tells us to seek first the Kingdom of God and His righteousness and all other things will be added to us (Matthew 6:33). God calls all believers to live for Him since He died for them! The challenge is that Jesus saved us to rule and reign over and in us as the one true King. Jesus exists in the heart and mind of the elect to show the compassionate act of God for all people. However, the compassion act of God requires one to be saved or requires access to the Kingdom through the spiritual Feast of Passover. Christ as the Passover Lamb established a new covenant wherein He fulfilled the requirements of the law and paid the debt for the sinner by dying for his sin. The power of God was realized in the bodily resurrection of Jesus, which demonstrated His power over death, death's sting, and the grave.

Jesus' resurrection demonstrated dominion over the god of this world, Satan, and the sovereignty of God in the spirit realm. Christ is King, not simply Savior, but if your perspective is that He is simply Savior, you will relate to Him out of a Savior model and not a Kingdom model. This is what has happened to many believers of Jesus Christ.

While Christ's mission most definitely provided a way of escape from eternal damnation and access to the Kingdom through His resurrection, that was not His sole purpose. He came to establish the Kingdom of God over the kingdom of Satan. Thus, His message and ministry were proclaiming the Kingdom, explaining the Kingdom, and demonstrating the Kingdom. He lived and taught the Kingdom, what it meant to be a citizen of the Kingdom, and how to abide under the reign of God as the Kingdom of God forcibly advances in this age. His death and resurrection were the means to be able to use human beings to also "seek and to save that which was lost" (Luke 19:10).

Jesus' message was focused upon the Kingdom age, which was the age to come, breaking into this present age. Hence, He inaugurated a clash of the kingdoms and demonstrated through the finger and power of God that He was superior to Satan, his principalities, and dominions. Jesus is not simply Savior – He is Lord and King!

This omission, I argue, is a weighty matter due to the fact that the church has severed Jesus from His Jewish roots. Separating Jesus from Judaism has caused the Christian church to prioritize its mission and ministry over His message – thus, we have changed the gospel! And if the gospel has been misfocused, under what pretense, have people been brought to Jesus Christ?

I pray that this book enlightens and causes you to rethink and refocus upon the Word of God. The truth in this book is not hidden; it has been there all along if we would open our eyes and see. The church must return to the gospel of the Kingdom – it is our destiny.

Dana Carson, BS, MS, M.Div., MBA, C.Psy.D., D.Min., Ph.D.

1

Why the Need for a Reformation of the Gospel?

Christians have an understanding of the gospel from their belief in Jesus Christ, His teachings, and the inspired writings of His disciples. Christianity, however, did not appear in modern history in a vacuum; those who first believed in Jesus Christ originated from a Middle Eastern community called "Israel" and a people called "Jews." Jesus was a Jew; He preached and taught from the Hebrew scriptures. Thus, the early Christians claimed that their beliefs were a direct offshoot of Judaism, the religion of the Jewish people. So, when Jesus and His people preached and taught about the "gospel," they had a context in which they understood what that meant. We are in dire need of a reformation of the "gospel," because what they understood and what we, the Christian church today, understands, are two very different things.

We believe that Jesus was and is the Messiah, the One who saves. Our understanding of Jesus as Messiah comes from the writers of the Newer Testament who proclaimed and taught that Jesus was the prophetic fulfillment of the promised Messiah. Good news, right? Yes and no. We are in need of a Kingdom reformation due to the lack of sound contextual teaching about Jesus the Messiah. We have taught Jesus from a European perspective and have missed the Jewishness of the scriptures that provide irreplaceable insights to the message, ministry, and mission of Christ. When we study the gospel in its authentic context, we better understand the claims, message, and expectations of Christ the King. We have grossly missed the Kingdom message; thus, we don't live for God – we seek to live off of God. People only know the saving grace of God; they do not know God as the One who desires to dominate their whole life.

Among the Jews, the understanding that the Messiah was to be the King of His people was common. Jesus was a Jew who studied the Torah, the Prophets, and the Writings; He was familiar with the Messianic hope of Israel. He understood that the hope and expectation of every Jew was that the Messiah would come and sit on the throne of David and liberate them from the oppressive treatment and rule of foreign powers. This was common knowledge in the original context of the gospel message of Christ.

It was this understanding that inspired the ancient wise men, who studied religion in general, to follow the star of David and seek out Him who was to be born King of the Jews. It was this belief that fueled the paranoia of King Herod and inspired his genocidal edict to assassinate all male children under the age of two in Bethlehem and its districts. Herod saw the young baby Jesus as a potential threat to His throne and tried to kill Him. Let's review a very important Kingdom passage that is only paid attention to during the season of the advent of Christ:

> *Now after Jesus was born in Bethlehem of Judea in the days of Herod the king, behold, wise men from the East came to Jerusalem, saying, "Where is He who has been born King of the Jews? For we have seen His star in the East and have come to worship Him." When Herod the king heard this, he was troubled, and all Jerusalem with him. And when he had gathered all the chief priests*

and scribes of the people together, he inquired of them where the Christ was to be born. So they said to him, "In Bethlehem of Judea, for thus it is written by the prophet:

'But you, Bethlehem, in the land of Judah,
Are not the least among the rulers of Judah;
For out of you shall come a Ruler
Who will shepherd My people Israel.' "

Then Herod, when he had secretly called the wise men, determined from them what time the star appeared. And he sent them to Bethlehem and said, "Go and search carefully for the young Child, and when you have found Him, bring back word to me, that I may come and worship Him also." When they heard the king, they departed; and behold, the star which they had seen in the East went before them, till it came and stood over where the young Child was. When they saw the star, they rejoiced with exceedingly great joy. And when they had come into the house, they saw the young Child with Mary His mother, and fell down and worshiped Him. And when they had opened their treasures, they presented gifts to Him: gold, frankincense, and myrrh. Then, being divinely warned in a dream that they should not return to Herod, they departed for their own country another way. Now when they had departed, behold, an angel of the Lord appeared to Joseph in a dream, saying, "Arise, take the young Child and His mother, flee to Egypt, and stay there until I bring you word; for Herod will seek the young Child to destroy Him." When he arose, he took the young Child and His mother by night and departed for Egypt, and was there until the death of Herod, that it might be fulfilled which was spoken by the Lord through the prophet, saying, "Out of Egypt I called My Son." Then Herod, when he saw that he was deceived by the wise men, was exceedingly angry; and he sent forth and put to death all the male children who were in Bethlehem and in all its districts, from two years old and under, according to the time which he had determined from the wise men. Then was fulfilled what was spoken by Jeremiah the prophet, saying:

"A voice was heard in Ramah,
Lamentation, weeping, and great mourning,

Rachel weeping for her children,
Refusing to be comforted, Because they are no more."

Now when Herod was dead, behold, an angel of the Lord appeared in a dream to Joseph in Egypt, saying, "Arise, take the young Child and His mother, and go to the land of Israel, for those who sought the young Child's life are dead." Then he arose, took the young Child and His mother, and came into the land of Israel. But when he heard that Archelaus was reigning over Judea instead of his father Herod, he was afraid to go there. And being warned by God in a dream, he turned aside into the region of Galilee. And he came and dwelt in a city called Nazareth, that it might be fulfilled which was spoken by the prophets, "He shall be called a Nazarene."
– Matthew 2:1-23[1]

This narrative is about a potential clash of the kingdoms. Herod was a vassal of the Roman Empire, which meant, though he was in authority in Jerusalem, he was under the rule and reign of the Roman Emperor. King Herod saw the birth of the Jewish Messiah as a major threat to his throne. Herod was considered a power-crazed man who was paranoid and cruel. So when he discovered that Jesus may be the Messiah, his corrupt nature tried to abort the prophecies of the Older Testament and kill the child in order to protect his own rule and reign. Thus, this narrative provides the unarguable fact that the context in which Jesus was born was a known context of a coming King who saves, not a Savior who happens to be King!

The Christian church has minimized and missed the gospel of a theocratic Kingdom and has settled for a democratic church with a gospel that proclaims Christ as simply Savior. The Bible states that Christ ascended back to the right hand of the Father, and is now sitting on the throne (Romans 8:34, Ephesians 1:20). Christ is the eternal King, who secured dominion over death, and has been given a name that is above all other names. At the name of Jesus, every knee will bow (Philippians 2:9-10). Why should every knee bow? Because bowing is what you do for the King, especially upon His ascendency. Christ is King! But the church has reduced Him to 'The Man upstairs' or the 'One who has my back,' not the One who dictates my

1 All scriptural references hereafter are derived from the New King James Version, 1982, Nashville: Thomas Nelson.

focus, actions, and behaviors. Christ is the literal, not theoretical, King; and as King, He rules, reigns, and dominates.

The tragedy today is that people are trapped in the tradition trap of the church, which not only dictates how we operate in the church, but how we see Christ. Meanwhile, Christ is on the outside knocking and asking, "If anyone hears My voice and opens the door, I will come in to him and dine with him, and he with Me" (Revelation 3:20). Note that He did not mention "the church;" just individuals who hear His voice. When all is said and done, there are only two strands of churches today: the wayward church (Laodicea) and the remnant church (Philadelphia). Christ reigns and rules through the remnant church, and He appeals to the wayward church. Jesus is not in the wayward church; scripture teaches us He is outside beckoning anyone who hears to come to Him. Unaware, some people are inside the "church," thinking that they are enjoying and celebrating salvation, but are doing so without the King.

> *Behold, I stand at the door and knock. If anyone hears My voice and opens the door, I will come in to him and dine with him, and he with Me. To him who overcomes I will grant to sit with Me on My throne, as I also overcame and sat down with My Father on His throne. – Revelation 3:20-21*

Verse 21 makes it clear that in the original context of Christ, His Kingship, was the cultural backdrop. In John's revelation, Christ overcame and sat on the throne; a throne is where a king sits and rules. What did Christ overcome? He overcame sin, death, and the grave (byproducts of the kingdom of Satan), and now sits on the throne with declared power, both in heaven and in earth (Matthew 28:18). The works of Christ qualified Him to be a King whose influence can be experienced in this realm through His embassy, the church.

Jesus' resurrection was the power of the Kingdom of God dominating the power of Satan and overturning his works of oppression. Christ's message was the reality of the Kingdom on earth and many explanations on how it functions. Christ announced the readiness of the Kingdom of God; that now was the time of liberation or Jubilee, and it was all happening through Him. He was liberating people from the power of Satan. Luke records Peter's message to the Gentiles in Rome and states:

> *Then Peter opened his mouth and said: "In truth I perceive that God shows no partiality. But in every nation whoever fears Him and works righteousness is accepted by Him. The word which God sent to the children of Israel, preaching peace through Jesus Christ— He is Lord of all— that word you know, which was proclaimed throughout all Judea, and began from Galilee after the baptism which John preached: how God anointed Jesus of Nazareth with the Holy Spirit and with power, who went about doing good and healing all who were oppressed by the devil, for God was with Him. And we are witnesses of all things which He did both in the land of the Jews and in Jerusalem, whom they killed by hanging on a tree. Him God raised up on the third day, and showed Him openly, not to all the people, but to witnesses chosen before by God, even to us who ate and drank with Him after He arose from the dead. And He commanded us to preach to the people, and to testify that it is He who was ordained by God to be Judge of the living and the dead. To Him all the prophets witness that, through His name, whoever believes in Him will receive remission of sins." – Acts 10:34-43*

Let's analyze Peter's message, since it contains the message, ministry, and mission of Jesus Christ. Peter's message to the household of Cornelius was that Christ was the prophesied Messiah who operated with the Holy Spirit and with power. He used His power to overturn the power of Satan, thus He liberated those whom Satan oppressed. The disciples were witnesses that Jesus truly was the Messiah because His resurrection was the ultimate proof of messiahship. Peter also stated that, as King, He will judge the living and the dead, and through His reign, He forgives the sins of those who believe in Him. Peter's ultimate premise was Jesus is the Messiah!

The church is in critical need of Kingdom reformation! The early church was the purest context for hearing and interpreting the message of Christ. After this era, the message of Christ had to endure the cultural contamination of the Roman Empire, European colonization, and racist Protestantism. This era of anti-Semitism and Gentile-to-Gentile discrimination began in the 4th century, and still exists today.

Matthew 16:21-23	*From that time Jesus began to show to His disciples that He must go to Jerusalem, and suffer many things from the elders and chief priests and scribes, and be killed, and be raised the third day. Then Peter took Him aside and began to rebuke Him, saying, "Far be it from You, Lord; this shall not happen to You!" But He turned and said to Peter, "Get behind Me, Satan! You are an offense to Me, for you are not mindful of the things of God, but the things of men."*
Matthew 17:22-23	*Now while they were staying in Galilee, Jesus said to them, "The Son of Man is about to be betrayed into the hands of men, and they will kill Him, and the third day He will be raised up." And they were exceedingly sorrowful.*
Matthew 20:17-19	*Now Jesus, going up to Jerusalem, took the twelve disciples aside on the road and said to them, "Behold, we are going up to Jerusalem, and the Son of Man will be betrayed to the chief priests and to the scribes; and they will condemn Him to death, and deliver Him to the Gentiles to mock and to scourge and to crucify. And the third day He will rise again."*
Mark 8:31-33	*And He began to teach them that the Son of Man must suffer many things, and be rejected by the elders and chief priests and scribes, and be killed, and after three days rise again. He spoke this word openly. Then Peter took Him aside and began to rebuke Him. But when He had turned around and looked at His disciples, He rebuked Peter, saying, "Get behind Me, Satan! For you are not mindful of the things of God, but the things of men."*

Mark 9:30-32	*Then they departed from there and passed through Galilee, and He did not want anyone to know it. For He taught His disciples and said to them, "The Son of Man is being betrayed into the hands of men, and they will kill Him. And after He is killed, He will rise the third day." But they did not understand this saying, and were afraid to ask Him.*
Mark 10:32-34	*Now they were on the road, going up to Jerusalem, and Jesus was going before them; and they were amazed. And as they followed they were afraid. Then He took the twelve aside again and began to tell them the things that would happen to Him: "Behold, we are going up to Jerusalem, and the Son of Man will be betrayed to the chief priests and to the scribes; and they will condemn Him to death and deliver Him to the Gentiles; and they will mock Him, and scourge Him, and spit on Him, and kill Him. And the third day He will rise again."*
Luke 9:21-22	*And He strictly warned and commanded them to tell this to no one, saying, "The Son of Man must suffer many things, and be rejected by the elders and chief priests and scribes, and be killed, and be raised the third day."*
Luke 9:43-45	*And they were all amazed at the majesty of God. But while everyone marveled at all the things which Jesus did, He said to His disciples, "Let these words sink down into your ears, for the Son of Man is about to be betrayed into the hands of men." But they did not understand this saying, and it was hidden from them so that they did not perceive it; and they were afraid to ask Him about this saying.*

Luke 18:31-34	*Then He took the twelve aside and said to them, "Behold, we are going up to Jerusalem, and all things that are written by the prophets concerning the Son of Man will be accomplished. For He will be delivered to the Gentiles and will be mocked and insulted and spit upon. They will scourge Him and kill Him. And the third day He will rise again." But they understood none of these things; this saying was hidden from them, and they did not know the things which were spoken.*
John 12:23-36	*But Jesus answered them, saying, "The hour has come that the Son of Man should be glorified. Most assuredly, I say to you, unless a grain of wheat falls into the ground and dies, it remains alone; but if it dies, it produces much grain. He who loves his life will lose it, and he who hates his life in this world will keep it for eternal life. If anyone serves Me, let him follow Me; and where I am, there My servant will be also. If anyone serves Me, him My Father will honor. "Now My soul is troubled, and what shall I say? 'Father, save Me from this hour'? But for this purpose I came to this hour. Father, glorify Your name." Then a voice came from heaven, saying, "I have both glorified it and will glorify it again." Therefore the people who stood by and heard it said that it had thundered. Others said, "An angel has spoken to Him." Jesus answered and said, "This voice did not come because of Me, but for your sake. Now is the judgment of this world; now the ruler of this world will be cast out. And I, if I am lifted up from the earth, will draw all peoples to Myself." This He said, signifying by what death He would die. The people answered Him, "We have heard from the law that the Christ remains forever; and how can You say, 'The Son of Man must be lifted up'? Who is this Son of Man?" Then Jesus said to them, "A little while longer the light is with you. Walk while you have the light, lest darkness overtake you; he who walks in darkness does not know where he is going. While you have the light, believe in the light, that you may become sons of light." These things Jesus spoke, and departed, and was hidden from them.*

These passages show that Jesus did not publicly teach the gospel of His death and resurrection. Jesus only discussed His redemptive mission in private with His disciples, and they still did not understand His mission. Yet, this is the "gospel," according to the contemporary church. This is preached, taught, shouted, and sung about in the Christian community. The gospel of the Kingdom has nothing to do with Christ's death and resurrection; it was simply the vehicle to inaugurate the rule, reign, and dominion of God through Christ Jesus.

How the Gospel Was Transformed

The contemporary church is in a sad situation, because it is primarily a Gentile church that really sees itself as superior to Judaism (both orthodox and Messianic), who in turn, don't have much respect for the Protestant churches due to their ignorance of Christianity's Jewish roots. Jesus was a Jew, who came to His own. His authenticity as a Jew was confirmed at His bar mitzvah at 12 when He taught in the synagogue. The Gentiles, who are non-Jewish, were ingrafted into the faith according to Paul in Romans 11:11-24.

> *I say then, have they stumbled that they should fall? Certainly not! But through their fall, to provoke them to jealousy, salvation has come to the Gentiles. Now if their fall is riches for the world, and their failure riches for the Gentiles, how much more their fullness! For I speak to you Gentiles; inasmuch as I am an apostle to the Gentiles, I magnify my ministry, if by any means I may provoke to jealousy those who are my flesh and save some of them. For if their being cast away is the reconciling of the world, what will their acceptance be but life from the dead? For if the first fruit is holy, the lump is also holy; and if the root is holy, so are the branches. And if some of the branches were broken off, and you, being a wild olive tree, were grafted in among them, and with them became a partaker of the root and fatness of the olive tree, do not boast against the branches. But if you do boast, remember that you do not support the root, but the root supports you.*
>
> *You will say then, "Branches were broken off that I might be grafted in." Well said. Because of unbelief they were broken off, and you stand by faith. Do not be haughty, but fear. For if God*

> *did not spare the natural branches, He may not spare you either. Therefore consider the goodness and severity of God: on those who fell, severity; but toward you, goodness, if you continue in His goodness. Otherwise you also will be cut off. And they also, if they do not continue in unbelief, will be grafted in, for God is able to graft them in again. For if you were cut out of the olive tree which is wild by nature, and were grafted contrary to nature into a cultivated olive tree, how much more will these, who are natural branches, be grafted into their own olive tree?*

Rejection of the Jewish faith has hindered the church's ability to fully comprehend the message of Jesus Christ, which was always universal and inclusive. The message of Christ was directly addressed to the Jewish people, but His conversation with the Samaritan woman (and through her, the Samaritan people), along with the Syrophoenician woman, demonstrates that Christ's Kingdom was not limited to the Jewish people. His Kingdom power was at work with the Roman centurion's servant (Matthew 8:5-13), the Syrophoencian's daughter (Matthew 15:21-28), and the Samaritan woman's past and present (John 4:1-26). God's desire had always been to save the world, not just a certain group of people, even though He began His redemptive process by cutting covenant with Israel first. If the church really understood the message of the Kingdom, preached first to the Jews then to the Gentiles, it would have slammed shut the door to racism and prejudice in contemporary Christianity.

Man was created in the image of God and charged with the task of being fruitful and multiplying. God's covenant with Abram stated that in Him all the nations of the world would be blessed:

> *Now the Lord had said to Abram:*
> *"Get out of your country,*
> *From your family*
> *And from your father's house,*
> *To a land that I will show you.*
> *I will make you a great nation;*
> *I will bless you*
> *And make your name great;*
> *And you shall be a blessing.*

I will bless those who bless you,
And I will curse him who curses you;
And in you all the families of the earth shall be blessed." – Genesis 12:1-3

God always intended to touch the world through His covenant with Abram. Every living person matters to God; the Bible proclaims that Jesus died for the world, not just the Jew (John 3:16). God is concerned with all of His creation; every soul belongs to God; every soul must obey His command; and every soul that does not will suffer the consequences:

"Behold, all souls are Mine;
The soul of the father
As well as the soul of the son is Mine;
The soul who sins shall die. – Ezekiel 18:4

When it comes to their relation to God, Jewish people may feel some superiority based on them being the chosen people of God. But God is the Lord of all, not just the Jew, but also the Gentile.

Indeed He says,
'It is too small a thing that You should be My Servant
To raise up the tribes of Jacob,
And to restore the preserved ones of Israel;
I will also give You as a light to the Gentiles,
That You should be My salvation to the ends of the earth.'" – Isaiah 49:6

When we study the scripture, we see God's intent to include the Gentiles when Saul of Tarsus, a Pharisee par excellence and Roman citizen, was called to be the true apostle to the Gentiles. Paul was a very strategic choice by God. A Jew trained in Judaism and Greek thought and philosophy, he was selected to be the apostle to the Gentiles and was inspired by God to write two-thirds of the Newer Testament for us. Paul's mission and message was one of inclusion, the Gentiles and Jews being called together to form the Body of Christ—the church (Ephesians 2:14-19).

Paul, however, was very conscious of the racial and cultural tension and division even within the Jewish community, to the point that he once confronted Peter about his struggle with Jewish prejudice and Gentile discrimination (Galatians 2:11-21). Paul was very sensitive to Gentile and Jewish relations. Paul himself was born a citizen of two kingdoms – Roman and Jewish. However, before he clashed with Peter, God sent Peter to the house of Cornelius, a Roman centurion, a Gentile. But before Peter went, God had to deal with his racial profiling and discrimination:

> *There was a certain man in Caesarea called Cornelius, a centurion of what was called the Italian Regiment, a devout man and one who feared God with all his household, who gave alms generously to the people, and prayed to God always. About the ninth hour of the day he saw clearly in a vision an angel of God coming in and saying to him, "Cornelius!" And when he observed him, he was afraid, and said, "What is it, lord?" So he said to him, "Your prayers and your alms have come up for a memorial before God. Now send men to Joppa, and send for Simon whose surname is Peter. He is lodging with Simon, a tanner, whose house is by the sea. He will tell you what you must do." And when the angel who spoke to him had departed, Cornelius called two of his household servants and a devout soldier from among those who waited on him continually. So when he had explained all these things to them, he sent them to Joppa.*
>
> *The next day, as they went on their journey and drew near the city, Peter went up on the housetop to pray, about the sixth hour. Then he became very hungry and wanted to eat; but while they made ready, he fell into a trance and saw heaven opened and an object like a great sheet bound at the four corners, descending to him and let down to the earth. In it were all kinds of four-footed animals of the earth, wild beasts, creeping things, and birds of the air. And a voice came to him, "Rise, Peter; kill and eat."*
>
> *But Peter said, "Not so, Lord! For I have never eaten anything common or unclean." And a voice spoke to him again the second time, "What God has cleansed you must not call common." This was done three times. And the object was taken up into heaven again. – Acts 10:1-16*

In Antioch, "almost the whole city" came to hear Paul and Barnabas preach the Word. This made the Jews very envious. So, Paul quoted Isaiah 49:6 to show how God had set him apart to preach the Word of God to the Gentiles, as He prophesied would happen. The Holy Spirit moved on them to receive the Word with gladness and sincerity en masse. The early church also had to come to grips with the fact that the same gift of the Holy Spirit, which Christ promised the Jews, was also poured out upon the Gentiles.

> *If therefore God gave them the same gift as He gave us when we believed on the Lord Jesus Christ, who was I that I could withstand God?" When they heard these things they became silent; and they glorified God, saying, "Then God has also granted to the Gentiles repentance to life." – Acts 11:17-18*

The Jewish believers in Christ had to get over their misconception and limited view of God's Kingdom being for the Jew alone, based upon their expectation of the restoration of a Jewish political kingdom modeled after King David. Thus, through proclamation, explanation, and demonstration, God showed the Jewish believers that Christ died for all people, not simply the Jews.

Now, what's amazing is the Gentile-to-Gentile prejudicial behavior in the church. It is absolutely ridiculous for Gentiles to exist in a relationship with God with an air of superiority, when the scriptures place us in the faith only upon the rejection of Christ by the Jews. It may not be right, but the only ethnic or religious group that has a historical basis to claim superiority with God is the Jew. However, scripture does not promote or prophesy a Jewish kingdom. The scriptures teach about the Kingdom of God, and in it, all the citizens are equal. God's Kingdom was intended to appeal to every ethnic group on the earth.

The Kingdom of God has absolutely no place for racial preference and superiority. Though Jesus was a Jew, Paul tells us that we should not focus on His fleshly origin, but His spiritual mission to make a new creation.

> *For the love of Christ compels us, because we judge thus: that if One died for all, then all died; and He died for all, that those who*

These passages show that Jesus did not publicly teach the gospel of His death and resurrection. Jesus only discussed His redemptive mission in private with His disciples, but they still did not understand it. Is this suggesting that the later teaching of Jesus' death and resurrection is at odds with His message of the Kingdom? No. The death and resurrection of Jesus was at the heart of apostolic preaching. Yet Luke notes that during his two-year Roman imprisonment, Paul continued "preaching the kingdom of God and teaching the things which concern the Lord Jesus Christ" (Acts 28:31).

The Resurrection of Jesus Christ

The resurrection of Jesus is vital and indispensable to the Kingdom message and mission of the church. Indeed, the Kingdom message and mission are incomplete without it. Clearly, Jesus could not have incorporated it in His teaching, because His resurrection was a future, culminating event of His earthly ministry.

There can be no doubt that in His ministry of preaching, teaching, and healing, Jesus showed that He was King of the Kingdom He came to establish. But it is clear throughout Acts and the epistles that He was anointed and crowned King at the resurrection with universal power over His enemies. In commissioning His disciples to world evangelization after His resurrection, He said, "All authority has been given to Me in heaven and on earth" (Matthew 28:18). Luke gives us an early sample of a recurring theme in Acts and what was the keynote of the early church's proclamation: through the resurrection and ascension, God has made Jesus both Lord and Christ (2:36).

Paul makes no less of the significance of Christ's resurrection. Listen to what he has to say about it: "[God] raised Him from the dead and seated Him at his right hand in the heavenly places, far above all principality and power and might and dominion, and every name that is named, not only in this age but also in that which is to come. And He put all things under His feet, and gave Him to be head over all things to the church" (Ephesians 1:20-22).

The seed of Jesus' Kingdom vision of God's universal reign inaugurated during His earthly ministry came to flower when Jesus was raised from the dead. At His resurrection, He was installed as King of kings and Lord of lords with universal power to accomplish His Kingdom purposes. His resurrection and ascension are evidence of His present reign. Thus, all hostile human and spiritual foes on earth or in the heavenlies must eventually surrender to Him. The resurrection message did not replace the Kingdom message, but expanded it and became central to it – the risen Christ, sending the Holy Spirit to empower believers to extend its reach globally through word and deed.

Christ did not publicize that He was the Messiah. He did not publicize His virgin birth; He did not even promote His own self-righteousness. He only proclaimed the Kingdom of God. I know this is difficult for some of you because you, like myself, have been taught your whole lives that the gospel was the good news of Jesus' death on a cross, burial in the borrowed tomb of Joseph, and third day resurrection. This was to become part of the good news, but only after the resurrection and ascension. Jesus' death and resurrection neither nullifies nor falsifies the Kingdom message; it strengthens it, for through the power of the Holy Spirit, the living, reigning Lord extends his Kingdom borders to the ends of the earth. Like Paul who placed the death and resurrection of Christ at the heart of Christian doctrine (1 Corinthians 15), yet preached the gospel of the Kingdom (Acts 28), so it is possible—even necessary—that the contemporary church proclaim the Kingdom message while not setting aside the death and resurrection of Christ.

Let's dig a little deeper so that you don't think I've lost it or have become a heretic and my teachings anathema.

> *Then Jesus went about all the cities and villages, teaching in their synagogues, preaching the gospel of the kingdom, and healing every sickness and every disease among the people. – Matthew 9:35*

> *Now when it was day, He departed and went into a deserted place. And the crowd sought Him and came to Him, and tried to keep Him from leaving them; but He said to them, "I must preach the*

> *kingdom of God to the other cities also, because for this purpose I have been sent." And He was preaching in the synagogues of Galilee. – Luke 4:42-44*

> *Now it came to pass, afterward, that He went through every city and village, preaching and bringing the glad tidings of the kingdom of God. And the twelve were with Him, and certain women who had been healed of evil spirits and infirmities—Mary called Magdalene, out of whom had come seven demons, and Joanna the wife of Chuza, Herod's steward, and Susanna, and many others who provided for Him from their substance. – Luke 8:1-3*

Each scriptural reference refers to Jesus preaching the good news or glad tidings of the Kingdom of God – this was the focal message of the ministry of Christ. Christ preached and taught the Kingdom of God, and He then demonstrated the Kingdom by taking authority over the works of Satan in the lives and bodies of people. So Christ's ministry consisted of proclamation, explanation, and demonstration of the Kingdom; He became the incarnate God for the express purpose of inaugurating the Kingdom of God.

The message of Christ focused upon the good news of the Kingdom of God. What is the good news or gospel? We can get a great deal of insight from examining the phrases "good news" or "gospel of the Kingdom." The term "gospel" in the Greek is *euaggelion* (εὐαγγέλιον) meaning "bringing good news," which is from *eú* meaning "good, well," and *aggéllo* meaning "to proclaim, tell." Originally, "gospel" meant "a reward for good news," but later became "good news." The Greek word for "kingdom" is *basileia* (βασιλεία); the cognate *basileus* means "king." Thus, "kingdom" means "royal dominion" (Matthew 4:8).

In the gospel according to Matthew, the phrase *Basileia tón ouranón,* "the Kingdom of heaven" or of the heavens, is more common (Matthew 3:2; 4:17; 5:3, 10, 19-20; 7:21; 8:11; 10:7; 11:11-12; 13:11, 24, 31, 33, 44-45, 47, 52; 16:19; 18:1, 3-4, 23; 19:12, 14, 23; 20:1; 22:2; 23:13; 25:1, 14). The other phrase used most commonly to describe the gospel that Jesus preached, primarily in the other gospels, is *Basileia tou Theou* or the "the Kingdom of God" (Mark 1:14-15; 4:11, 26, 30; 9:1, 47; 10:14-15, 23-25;

12:34; 14:25; 15:43, Luke 4:43; 6:20; 7:28; 8:1, 10; 9:2, 11, 27, 60, 62; 10:9, 11; 11:20; 12:31; 13:18, 20, 28-29; 14:15; 16:16; 17:20-21; 18:16-17, 24-25, 29; 19:11; 21:31; 22:16, 18; 23:51, John 3:3, 5). In an attempt to not take the name of the Lord in vain, Matthew, due to his deep Jewish roots, tended to avoid using the name of God, using "Kingdom of heaven" instead. Matthew also used the phrase, "Kingdom of God," but was very strategic in His usage of the phrase (Matthew 6:33; 12:28; 19:24; 21:31, 43). The two phrases, "Kingdom of God" and "Kingdom of heaven," essentially mean the same thing and can be used interchangeably (Matthew 19:23-24).

The Kingdom of God is the rule and reign of God in the realm of a man's heart that brings him to total submission to the will of God (Luke 17:21). Both expressions, "Kingdom of God" and "Kingdom of heaven," hark back to the prophecies of Daniel (2:44; 7:14) and denote the everlasting Kingdom that God the Father will give to Christ the Son. Namely, the Father will bestow the spiritual and eternal Kingdom, which is to exist first in more imperfect circumstances on earth, but afterwards will appear complete in the world of glory (Matthew 25:31-46, Mark 13:26-27, Luke 21:27-28).

Since "Kingdom" may carry a temporal, spatial, spiritual, existential, and/or eschatological meaning, it must be interpreted in context. Its uses above should be understood as the rule that God establishes in the hearts of men when Jesus Christ is received by faith, but also the eschatological future Kingdom to be established in the hereafter, during which the believers will reign with Christ forever (Revelation 22:1-5). In the above references, however, when it is the gospel of the Kingdom of God or the eternal gospel, reference is to the invisible rule of Christ in the hearts of believers.

Let's look closer at the concept of the Kingdom. The gospel of the Kingdom is the good news of God's reign. When I use the term "reign," it suggests that it is the period of time when God actively utilizes His authority or rule. Jesus came to inaugurate the rule and reign of God in the hearts of men. He did so by preaching the rule, teaching the rule, and demonstrating the rule. Jesus demonstrated the power and authority of the Kingdom of God by casting out demons, healing the sick, performing miracles, and raising the dead. He demonstrated dominion through the exercise of His kingly power. The Kingdom of God speaks of the spiritual Kingdom and the glorious reign of the Messiah. The idea of the Kingdom has its basis in the prophecies of the Older Testament where the coming of the Messiah and His triumphs are foretold (Psalm 2; 110, Isaiah 2:1-4; 11:1, Jeremiah 23:5; 31:31; 32:37; 33:14, Ezekiel 34:23; 37:24, Micah 4:1, and especially Daniel 2:44; 17:14, 27; 9:25).

The Messiah's reign is described as a golden age when true righteousness will be established, and His theocratic structure will usher in peace and happiness. The Jews interpreted these prophecies with a temporal meaning and expected a Messiah who would come in the clouds of heaven. As king of the Jewish people, He was expected to restore the ancient Jewish religion and worship, reform the corrupt morals of the people, make expiation for their sins, give freedom from the yoke of foreign dominion, and at length, reign over the whole earth in peace and glory. This is made evident by the post-resurrection conversation that Luke records in the book of Acts:

> *And being assembled together with them, He commanded them not to depart from Jerusalem, but to wait for the Promise of the Father, "which," He said, "you have heard from Me; for John truly baptized with water, but you shall be baptized with the Holy Spirit not many days from now." Therefore, when they had come together, they asked Him, saying, "Lord, will You at this time restore the Kingdom to Israel?" And He said to them, "It is not for you to know times or seasons which the Father has put in His own authority. But you shall receive power when the Holy Spirit has come upon you; and you shall be witnesses to Me in Jerusalem, and in all Judea and Samaria, and to the end of the earth." – Acts 1:4-8*

The gospel of the Kingdom is the good news of God's reign, which is the message that Christ preached, taught, and demonstrated. Christ was totally consumed with the gospel of the Kingdom during His earthly ministry and post-resurrection:

> *...until the day in which He was taken up, after He through the Holy Spirit had given commandments to the apostles whom He had chosen, to whom He also presented Himself alive after His suffering by many infallible proofs, being seen by them during forty days and speaking of the things pertaining to the kingdom of God.* – Acts 1:2-3

The scripture states that even after the resurrection, He was not preaching, "I told you I would get up." Instead, Jesus was teaching and explaining the things concerning the Kingdom. His crucifixion and resurrection simply authenticated the claims of His Messiahship.

The message of Jesus was the gospel of the Kingdom. Jesus came teaching a gospel that not only involved the loss of His life, but a gospel that demands that we lose our lives.

> *When He had called the people to Himself, with His disciples also, He said to them, "Whoever desires to come after Me, let him deny himself, and take up his cross, and follow Me. For whoever desires to save his life will lose it, but whoever loses his life for My sake and the gospel's will save it. For what will it profit a man if he gains the whole world, and loses his own soul? Or what will a man give in exchange for his soul? For whoever is ashamed of Me and My words in this adulterous and sinful generation, of him the Son of Man also will be ashamed when He comes in the glory of His Father with the holy angels." – Mark 8:34-38*

Christ's message of the Kingdom declared that God was taking over the spiritual landscape of all of creation and inaugurating His Kingdom through His Son. Christ's message required people to abandon their desire to gain the world or be satisfied by the niceties of the world. Christ's message of the Kingdom addressed those who were under the influence and domination of Satan, declaring that through the gospel of the Kingdom, a person has the opportunity for liberation and Kingdom citizenship. Thus, Christ states:

> *The law and the prophets were until John. Since that time the kingdom of God has been preached, and everyone is pressing into*

it. And it is easier for heaven and earth to pass away than for one tittle of the law to fail. – Luke 16:16-17

Christ postulated that John the baptizing one began preaching the dispensation of the Kingdom of God, and people are pressing their way in through the mission of Christ. He healed the sick and rebuked demonic forces; and at the end, He redeemed mankind. Thus, His message of the Kingdom was "God is King now!" And THAT is the gospel or good news – the power of God is overtaking the power of Satan! The miracles of Jesus demonstrate that the reign of God can be experienced. God is King now, and He reigns among His people who embrace His authority and experience His power. The Kingdom of God is God's unstoppable power at work, doing what it pleases. However, the Kingdom demands decision and urgent action; it requires that people submit to God and embrace His sovereignty in every area of their lives.

- **Christ's Message** *was the Kingdom of God!*
- **Christ's Ministry** *was Deliverance and Liberation as the Promised Messiah!*
- **Christ's Mission** *was Redemption as the Lamb of God!*

The reign of God must be experienced by the people of God who obey His Word. The Kingdom of God was the principal reason and cause for which Jesus lived and died. Dr. Trevor Grizzle, my dear friend and colleague, states:

> "By preaching, Jesus announced the message of the Kingdom of God; by teaching, He explained its meaning and character; by healing and miracles, He demonstrated its presence and power in the world."[1]

1 Carson, Dana. (2012), *The Kingdom, the Church, and You*, Alvin, TX: Dana Carson Kingdom Ministries.

Please note this was BEFORE His death, burial, and resurrection. In fact, the Matthean gospel states that the gospel was being preached to the poor, and the power and authority of the King was setting the captives free from their infirmities.

> *Jesus answered and said to them, "Go and tell John the things which you hear and see: The blind see and the lame walk; the lepers are cleansed and the deaf hear; the dead are raised up and the poor have the gospel preached to them. And blessed is he who is not offended because of Me." – Matthew 11:4-6*

Jesus preached the Kingdom – not "be born again" or His death, burial, and resurrection. In fact, in all four gospels, the subject matter of being born again is only mentioned once. The topic of being born again was not the message of the Kingdom; but it was a topic of interest for Nicodemus, the Pharisee, so he asked Jesus. Jesus' response to Nicodemus was that the only way to experience the Kingdom of God and the hope of the Messiah is to be born from above.

> *Jesus answered and said to him, "Most assuredly, I say to you, unless one is born again, he cannot see the kingdom of God." Nicodemus said to Him, "How can a man be born when he is old? Can he enter a second time into his mother's womb and be born?" Jesus answered, "Most assuredly, I say to you, unless one is born of water and the Spirit, he cannot enter the kingdom of God. That which is born of the flesh is flesh, and that which is born of the Spirit is spirit. Do not marvel that I said to you, 'You must be born again.' The wind blows where it wishes, and you hear the sound of it, but cannot tell where it comes from and where it goes. So is everyone who is born of the Spirit." – John 3:3-8*

This is the only place in John's gospel that this concept is mentioned; but it was never a sermon He preached from town to town or a parabolic teaching he taught the multitudes. Jesus simply stated a fact about how one sees and enters the Kingdom. He gave special advice to a Pharisee who desired to become a part of the Kingdom. While the topic of spiritual conversion or new birth is most certainly a major biblical theme that can be traced from the Older to the Newer Testament, it is not the gospel of the Kingdom. The reign of God is connected to redemption and salvation, because being born from above is a means to an end. In order to become a part of God's Kingdom, you MUST be born into the Kingdom, which indicates citizenship. After Christ established that Kingdom citizenship requires being born again, He then declared that those who are born again lose control of their lives and are directed by the sovereign King.

What confuses a lot of modern believers is the distinction of the good news of Christ's miraculous virgin birth, sinless life, death on the cross, and resurrection from the dead vs. the reign and rule of God inaugurated in Christ Jesus. Though the mission of Christ was the redemption of mankind, it is not the Kingdom message nor was redemption His end goal. How do we know? Christ continued to teach the disciples about the Kingdom of God after the resurrection (Acts 1:3-6). The authentic message of Jesus was the gospel of the Kingdom – the good news that God can become your King, you do not have to continue to be oppressed by the devil! Then, He fulfilled the Jewish rite of atonement for humanity – personally sponsoring a Kingdom citizenship program through faith in Him. The ministry of Christ is liberation; thus, He states:

> *"The Spirit of the Lord is upon Me,*
> *Because He has anointed Me*
> *To preach the gospel to the poor;*
> *He has sent Me to heal the brokenhearted,*
> *To proclaim liberty to the captives*
> *And recovery of sight to the blind,*
> *To set at liberty those who are oppressed;*
> *To proclaim the acceptable year of the Lord."*
> *Then He closed the book, and gave it back to the attendant and sat down.*
> *And the eyes of all who were in the synagogue were fixed on Him.*
> *And He began to say to them, "Today this Scripture is fulfilled in your hearing." – Luke 4:18-21*

When you examine the gospels and study the ministry of Christ, you will see that this is reflective of what Christ did when He was here in the flesh. He said, "Today," not after His resurrection, these scriptures would be fulfilled. He came preaching the gospel of jubilee or the acceptable year of God's favor. In essence, His statement meant that you can now enter the Kingdom – Jew and Gentile – through the mission of Jesus Christ. Thus, the anointing of Jesus could be summed up in these four words: proclamation, explanation, demonstration, and invitation. His death and resurrection were the invitation for He was the Passover Lamb and the Firstfruits. Through His death, He paid the debt of sin. Through His resurrection, He provided the keys to the Kingdom and made us partakers of the divine nature.

While entrance into the Kingdom is impossible without the death, burial, and bodily resurrection of Jesus, those events alone do not constitute the gospel of the Kingdom. The resurrection and ascension is proof of His present reign. It is good news that Christ died, was buried, and rose on the third day, but it is not the gospel of the Kingdom that Jesus preached. He came preaching Kingship, and His mission provided a way to citizenship. Today, many people know Him as Savior, but not as King or Lord. They realize that Jesus died for the sinner, but what they don't realize is that the sinner must die for Jesus. On Judgment Day, it will be a sad situation when some people discover that they are barred from entering the Kingdom, because they did not make Christ King. Some, in false allegiance, claimed Him to be Savior, but they never allowed Him to have the reins of their lives.

Consider this passage:

> *"Not everyone who says to Me, 'Lord, Lord,' shall enter the kingdom of heaven, but he who does the will of My Father in heaven. Many will say to Me in that day, 'Lord, Lord, have we not prophesied in Your name, cast out demons in Your name, and done many wonders in Your name?' And then I will declare to them, 'I never knew you; depart from Me, you who practice lawlessness!' – Matthew 7:21-23*

Such are the people Jesus refers to in Matthew 7 – people who, to be sure, were intimately aware of the Kingdom of God from a Jewish perspective and who were anticipating the Messiah, people who would say they knew

Him. But because they did not submit their wills to God and allow Him to reign in their hearts, they were disqualified from entry into the Kingdom.

I once heard a Messianic Jewish minister speaking on this verse. He stated that if the Jewish covenant is broken, then the covenant is regarded to have never existed. Thus, Christ was saying to those who did not submit to the will of the King that they were not Kingdom citizens; thus, they could not enter the Kingdom. The covenant had been broken, and now, it was as if a covenant never existed. Christ's message is that God desires to be your King; His ministry demonstrated the power to deliver and set the captive free, and His mission redeemed us from the curse of the law.

The rabbinic parables provide insight to Jewish thought and the teachings of Christ to modern Christians. Dr. Young cites a rabbinic parable concerning the deeper spiritual meaning of the Kingdom of heaven and the exodus of the slaves from Egypt. The parable goes as follows:

> "To what may the matter be compared? To one who came to a province, and said to the people, 'May I reign over you?' They said to him, 'You have done nothing good for us that we should accept your reign.' What did he do? He built them a wall. He brought them water. He fought battles for them. Then he said to them, 'May I reign over you?' They responded, 'Yes! Yes!' Thus, it was with the Omnipresent One; He redeemed Israel from Egypt. He parted the Red Sea for them. He rained manna from heaven, He provided them a well, and He sent quail. He fought the battle of Amalek for them. He said to them, 'May I reign over you?', and they replied, 'Yes! Yes!' The rabbi teaches, 'This shows the grace of Israel. When they stood before Mount Sinai to receive Torah, they all determined in their hearts to accept the kingdom with joy.'" – *Ancient Jewish Bible Commentary, Midrash, Mekilta on Exodus 15.*[2]

2 Dr. Brad Young. *Paul, the Jewish Theologian*, Hendrickson Pub (November, 1, 1997).

When you consider that He became man for us, He became sin for us, He taught us, He died for us, He was raised from the dead for us, He is coming back for us; the question is – can He reign over you? The answer should be, "Yes! Yes!"

God / Jesus
became a man for us
To become SIN for us.

Spiritual Organism: A family of which
God is a part and we are in a spiritual
relationship, gradually taking on the
characteristics of Him.

Church is the Body of Christ

Resurrected body

We are to communicate
The Gospel of the Kingdom
Through relationship.

Organism of our faith
One faith - one hope one baptism one God
one savior one life (life of Christ)
Organism spiritual gifts

3

Seven Dispensations of Theological Renewal

If you are like most people to whom I have shared this illumination, by now, you might be asking, how did this happen in God's church? Why isn't the church preaching this message? I thought the same thing. So, after much study, prayer, and analysis by other scholars of the Word, I developed a historical timeline to explain this phenomenon. This section is designed to help you understand how Satan methodically removed the universal message of the Kingdom, couched within the culture of the Jews, and replaced it with the message of the church, making the church a social institution rather that a spiritual organism of the Kingdom of God. The change has occurred over time, thus the answers we seek can only be found by examining history. Looking at the church historically from a doctrinal perspective, you must consider the concept of "dispensation" from a doctrinal perspective in order to demonstrate what happened to the message of the Kingdom.

For this cause, I developed, what I refer to as, the Seven Dispensations of Theological Renewal[1] that parallel the progression of the church age:

1. Revelation
2. Identification
3. Salvation
4. Regeneration
5. Impartation
6. Participation
7. Exaltation

I began looking at these seven epochs of times/seasons of the church age and examined the church's teachings over the last 2,000 years since her birth. Let's begin examining the church eras and discover where the Kingdom message began and strayed and then returned.

1. The Dispensation of Revelation

The early church was given the most comprehensive understanding of the gospel of the Kingdom and the mission of Christ. The early church gleaned from eyewitnesses, the disciples, and the teachings of Christ on the Kingdom. The disciples were extremely important in ensuring that the message that they heard and saw was spread throughout the world. The disciples were not operating out of hearsay; they were actual eyewitnesses who experienced the ministry of Jesus firsthand and who were trained by Jesus Himself (Acts 4:20). The gospels give us detailed narratives of the life, mission, and teachings of Christ, as witnessed by His disciples. The book of Acts demonstrates how the disciples (later the apostles) executed what Christ commissioned them to do for His Kingdom. The early church not only benefited from the teaching of the disciples, but the Gentiles as well; the disciples presided on the Jerusalem Council concerning the integration of the Gentiles into the believing community. With this tremendous revelation, the early church practiced the most powerful representation of the call and cause of Christ that we know. Thus, the gospels and the book of Acts serve as a historical record of the intended focus and scope of the mission of the church and its teachings.

1 Carson, Dana. (2008), *The Doors of the Church Are Closed*, Alvin, TX: Xulon Press.

I refer to this era as the Dispensation of Revelation, because this was the era in which the Holy Spirit inspired men to write the Word of God. I want to make sure I emphasize the preeminence I give to the Word of God. The Bible is not given to us by interpretation; thus, it has no errors. Men, assigned to provide the world with the wisdom of God, penned the Bible through God-breathed inspiration (1 Timothy 3:16). If anyone or any era contained a holistic understanding of the Word of God, it was the 1st century saints and the early church. The early church was the first and only dispensation in which the mind of God was understood concerning His Kingdom, the church, and the world. The time span for the early church was from Pentecost through the 3rd century. This church actually laid the foundation for the gospel to be preached upon every continent. This church witnessed the excellencies of Christ from Jerusalem to the uttermost parts of the world! Its members understood their mission, the methodology, their mandate, and their message! Thus, they were willingly persecuted, dispersed, and martyred for their faith.

2. The Dispensation of Identification

This dispensation was both a blessing and a curse. This dispensation was birthed in the 4th century upon the cessation of Christian persecution with the signing of the Edict of Milan. This official document ended Christian persecution and allowed Christians to freely practice their faith. During this era, Christianity became the official religion of the Roman Empire. After decades of persecution, to be a Roman citizen was to be a Christian and to be a Christian was to be a Roman citizen. Roman and Christian was synonymous in nomenclature. With the freedom to practice Christianity, void of the fear and threat of persecution and death, the church could now attend to unfinished business. However, since Christianity became the official religion of Rome, there was no need for the church to fulfill the Great Commission, which was the final command of Christ. The entire Roman Empire automatically became Christian upon baptism as infants.

This era opened the 'doors of the church,' rather than unlock the 'doors to the Kingdom'! The Roman Empire, led by the influence of Constantine the Great, opened the doors of the church and everyone became a member. Conversion became unnecessary in this new Christian religion. The empire thought that one of the highest privileges the church could have ever been given was Roman legitimacy, because the Roman Empire was believed to be one of the most advanced and superior empires in the world. Gone was study in the Temple; gone was house-to-house worship; gone was communal giving; gone was Kingdom fellowship; gone was public testimonies and exhortations; and gone were the signs and wonders. The marriage between the state and the church damaged the Christian church forever!

The blessing that came out this era was the peace and tranquility the church experienced, which allowed the collection of all the writings of the apostles. Church leaders, inspired to compile, copy, and translate the Bible, gathered in 397 AD at the Council of Carthage to compile the first canon of the Newer Testament. Prior to collecting all of the writings, this era was famously known for its church doctrine councils. These councils were designed to decide what would be the official doctrines of Christianity. These councils would convene and rigorously argue and debate scripture and theological controversies. Several renowned theological thinkers, commonly referred to as the patristics or early church fathers, emerged from these councils. Many of them, originating from Northern Africa, became known for developing the primary doctrines of the church formally summarized in church creeds. Some of the most important creeds that came out of these councils were: the Nicene Creed, the Constantinople Creed, the Athanasian Creed, and the Apostles' Creed. Also among these councils were Chalcedon and Ephesus, which were very instrumental during the Dispensation of Identification.

Why do I refer to this era as the Dispensation of Identification? The Dispensation of Identification allowed the church to fully identify who Christ is in relationship to God the Father and God the Holy Spirit. During this era, Christ was declared *homoousia* or "of the same substance" as God. After careful study of the scriptures, the Council of Nicaea declared Christ as fully God and fully man, not confounding or mixing the two natures of Christ. This is the dispensation in which a great deal of attention was given to the Trinity – one God in three Persons. Our present-day understanding of Christ as both Lord and Savior, God, and man developed during this era, which was marked by such great thinkers as Athanasius, St. Augustine,

Origen, Tertullian, Chrysostom, Cyprian, the three Cappadocians, and others. This era extended from the 4th century through the 16th century.

3. The Dispensation of Salvation

This period, beginning in the 1500s, is called the era of the pre-Reformation movement. During this period, the theology of the Roman Catholic Church was beginning to be challenged by men such as John Wycliffe and John Huss. The Reformation period culminated under the efforts of Martin Luther, who had an experience that caused him to re-examine the scriptures concerning what the church taught about eternal life and how one obtains eternal life. Luther disagreed with measures the church required people to perform in order to please God (works righteousness) and secure their dead loved ones' rightstanding with Him. Luther's research led him to conclude that salvation cannot be granted by the Roman Catholic Church or through penance or prayers for the dead. The way to salvation, Luther determined, was *sola fide* (by faith alone), *sola gratia* (by grace alone), *sola scriptura* (by scripture alone), and *solus Christus* (by Christ alone). Luther challenged Roman Catholic scholars to an open theological debate concerning salvation by nailing his 95 Theses or theological statements on the door of the church of Wittenberg in 1517.

His theses condemned their teachings, so of course that did not go over very well with the Roman Catholic officials. Luther never got a chance to debate his positions, but had to be hurried out of the city and placed in hiding. He became a wanted man for concluding that you did not need to embrace the traditions of the Roman Catholic Church in order to have a relationship with Christ, but simply believe the scriptures and receive salvation as a free gift given by God in Christ. Luther's protest concerning the Roman Catholic Church was the catalyst for the first movement away from Roman Catholicism. In this era, the first Protestant denominations were formed – the Lutherans, Calvinists (Presbyterians, Reformed churches), Anglicanism, and the Anabaptists. Interestingly, Luther was not attempting to shut the doors of the Roman Catholic Church; he was simply challenging the church to rethink its teachings.

Luther's treatises serve as the basis for our soteriology or doctrine of salvation. Luther was not a lone ranger in this endeavor – other men, such as John Calvin and Ulrich Zwingli, also challenged Roman Catholicism and its lack of biblical basis for its beliefs and practices. The Dispensation of Salvation covered the 1500s and the 1600s. Wow! Consider this: over 1,000 years after Christ and the only thing the church reclaimed since the 1st century was who He is and the requirements of salvation.

4. The Dispensation of Regeneration

This dispensation has its roots in the English Reformation. The study of English Protestantism and Roman Catholicism is a very interesting historical investigation for those of you who enjoy soap operas. The official religion of England depended upon the religious views of the king or queen that was in office. The changing of the guards was always accompanied with drama. However, one of the greatest reformers and preachers who ever lived came out of this era in the 1700s, a man by the name of John Wesley. Wesley was a tremendous preacher who has been called the father of the Methodist church. He was an itinerant preacher who traveled around the country preaching the gospel. He could have been what some would refer to as a fire and brimstone preacher. His message focused upon regeneration; he was instrumental in reinstituting the message of regeneration in the church. He boldly proclaimed, "You must be born again!"

He and his brother Charles Wesley and other powerful English preachers, were instrumental in heralding the message of regeneration for two centuries. John and Charles Wesley, George Whitefield, and others were also instrumental in influencing religious groups, like the Quakers and the Puritans, toward religious pietism. Wesley focused upon ensuring that people had the internal witness of the Spirit of God to confirm that they were children of God. I refer to the 18th and 19th century as the Dispensation of Regeneration, because during this period, the message of conversion was preached and embraced. Wesley stressed the spiritual experience; he saw the need for believers to have two encounters with God, salvation and perfect love, because both were acts of grace. Wesley's fervor earned him the unofficial title of primary founder of the "you-must-be-born-again" movement, which was the flagship of the Great Awakening or the revivalist era in which Jonathan Edwards, George Whitefield, John and Charles Wesley, D.L. Moody, Charles Spurgeon were drum majors in England, Scotland, and America. In America, the Great Awakening produced the message of rejuvenation and gave birth to the first black Baptist church in mid-18th century – Silver Bluff Baptist Church of Aiken County, South Carolina.

5. The Dispensation of Impartation

This is the dispensation of what has been called the baptism in the Holy Spirit, evidenced by glossolalic speech, or "tongues." This dispensation was an extremely important dispensation marked by the number five, which is the number of grace. This dispensation gave birth to the re-visitation of the Holy Spirit after His first baptism of the disciples in the Upper Room. While this dispensation probably represents one of the most controversial within the Protestant Movement, it served as the catalyst for worldwide ministry. The baptism in the Holy Spirit was the dispensation in which the Spirit came to help unify and empower God's people for service.

This Dispensation of Impartation began during the time when Professor C. Carroll launched his work, *The Negro: A Beast or in the Image of God?*, a purported scientific and theological project that would educate Americans about the place of Negros in American society based on their nature. In the book, Carroll stated that blacks belong to the animal kingdom (beasts) and were created on the fifth day.

Paradoxically, the era had its watershed moment in a meeting where God poured out His Spirit on a group of people of color worshiping in California, evidenced by demonstrations of the power of the Holy Spirit that drew people of all races to these gatherings and ignited His people for ministry. A one-eyed black man named William J. Seymour led the gatherings, having learned about the baptism of the Holy Spirit, with the evidence of speaking in tongues, from a white gentleman by the name of Charles Parham. Historians suggest that Parham, who was a KKK sympathizer, never experienced glossolalic speech. The Holy Spirit was first believed to have fallen upon one of Parham's students, Agnes Ozman. After reports of the Holy Spirit falling upon the house church that Seymour pastored spread, the movement began to catch the attention of the world. The normative experience of speaking in other tongues in the early church was not known in our contemporary context until the 1800s in Great Britain under the leadership of Edward Irving and the Catholic Apostolic Church of Scotland and then, later, in the United States on Azusa Street in 1906.

The Holy Spirit fell heavy upon the services, and people not only spoke in other tongues, but exhibited other manifestations in the meetings on Bonnie Brae St. The church later moved to Azusa Street and, as the young people say, it was 'off the chain.' People were experiencing the baptism of the Holy Spirit for the empowerment of service and the unification of God's people. Unfortunately, the movement did not unite God's people, but further divided them along the lines of race and class. Racism and hatred were too prominent for whites to identify with blacks, even in church. Society deemed the entire movement heretical. Later, the movement slowly began to be identified with the rigidity of the Holiness Movement and the classism of the Assemblies of God.

Due to racism and the lack of sound biblical doctrine, the Dispensation of Impartation had minimal effect upon the black church in America, though its effects were felt worldwide. The Charismatic Movement was birthed in this era, and continues today as the most vital and vibrant aspect of the Body of Christ, crossing denominational lines, racial lines, and geographical lines. The baptism in the Holy Spirit is a global phenomenon of the Spirit.

6. The Dispensation of Participation

This era covers what has been called the Pentecostal/Charismatic/Full Gospel Movements. These movements have been instrumental in laying the foundation for layman engaging in their faith and participating in worship. These movements gave birth to prayer ministries, such as "Can ye not tarry for one hour?" by Dr. Larry Lea. They gave rise to an emphasis on studying the scriptures and trusting God according to His Word, teachings on spiritual warfare and seed sowing for blessings, and the praise and worship movement that created a new genre of interactive music, praise dancing, and the integration of the fine arts in worship.

Six, in biblical numerology, is the number of man. Thus, this dispensation of theological renewal was the one wherein emphasis was placed on the individual's active participation in worship. This was something totally different from Roman Catholicism and the mainline churches in the European church world. The 6th dispensation was the era in which people were allowed to personally express their faith, the formality of religion was subtly abandoned, the need for formally trained clergy diminished, and an emphasis on Bible training was replaced with experience. This was the era when people stopped saying 'the Bible states' and exchanged biblical authority for spiritual experience. The new buzz words became, 'the Spirit said to me' and 'the Holy Ghost taught me.' Laymen no longer demanded that their leaders be trained in the Word; and the number of men and women who desired to pastor denominational churches, which traditionally demanded trained leaders, declined.

So this dispensation produced a generation of 'ignorant pulpits': men and women, who taught simply from inspiration, totally void of information through education. Please don't get me wrong: not everyone has to go to seminary, but everyone, who is called to pastor or preach, must sit under someone who has been trained at some level in order to properly interpret the Word of God. Even Paul, who knew the law, trained under Gamaliel after his conversion and call to be Christ's messenger.

This era became not only a dispensation wherein men engaged their faith, but also went to extremes – to the point of no biblical accountability, contributing to the spiritual climate we experience now – rise in pride, insecurity, arrogance, and spiritual deception due to a lack of a firm theological education.

Let's re-cap the dispensations before we go to what is the final dispensation of theological renewal:

1. Revelation	The early church (Comprehensive understanding of the mission, mandate, methodology, and the message of Christ and His Kingdom)
2. Identification	The Roman Empire/Imperial Church (Who is Christ in relationship to the Triune God and man)
3. Salvation	The Reformation (How is one saved)
4. Regeneration	The Great Awakening (You must be born again)
5. Impartation	The Azusa Outpouring (Empowerment for service and unity)
6. Participation	The Pentecostal/Charismatic/Full Gospel Movements (Engaging one's faith at every level)

7. The Dispensation of Exaltation

The dispensation we live in today is the Dispensation of the Kingdom of God. After years of progressing in our knowledge of God, from the 4th century to the 20th century, believers are finally being challenged to focus upon the proclamation, explanation, and demonstration of the Kingdom of God – the things Christ focused on and the things the early church taught. In this dispensation, truly Holy Spirit-filled people will abandon the banner of traditionalism and reject the sociological church, the wayward or lukewarm church. As Paul warned Titus, "they profess to know God, but in works they deny Him, being abominable, disobedient, and disqualified for every good work" (Titus 1:16). Paul admonished Timothy to stay away from them (2 Timothy 3:5). There are people who have learned to enjoy church without Christ and they have been doing it so long, they no longer have the ability to recognize that He is no longer present in the building as King. However, Christ has a people who will come out from those who have a form of godliness, but deny the power and become a part of the church that received no condemnation from Christ in the book of Revelation – Philadelphia.

The scripture declares the Kingship of Christ or Christ as Messiah sitting on a throne. Christ's incarnation indicated His Kingship and Kingdom. Christ's presence upon the earth, while redemptive in nature, was royal in reality; He is King! Christ came to make Kingdom citizens through regeneration and discipleship. This is the dispensation where God's people – the true church – will again know and obey Jesus Christ as Master and sovereign Ruler.

Jesus' primary message, heralded by John the baptizer, and disseminated through the apostles and the 1st century church, was the Kingdom of God (or Kingdom of heaven). The Kingdom of God is the manifestation into which Christians are reborn through their salvific experience (John 3:3, 5). At salvation, a sinner becomes a Kingdom citizen, one who is no longer under the primary rule of the 'king of this world'. Living this kind of life requires that you understand what you came out of, how your life operated before salvation, what you have accepted as your new life in Christ's Kingdom, and how your spiritual life should be governed from now on. True Kingdom citizenship will lead to a re-prioritization of everything formally associated with your existence; redeemed, thus re-purposed.

Therefore, it is during this day and time that God is bringing the message of the Kingdom back to the forefront of His church. The good news of God's Kingdom is now breaking its way into the lives of people all across the world, and those who are entering the Kingdom are breaking out with its power. It is during this despensation that Christ will return for His church and ultimately do away with this age, ushering in the age to come – the Kingdom.

The 4th Century - The Final Nail

In the previous chapter, we discussed the Seven Dispensations of Theological Renewal, which I created to help you understand how the Kingdom message was proclaimed by Christ in the 1st century. However, the 1st century church eventually lost the Kingdom message and focus. In this chapter, we will discuss in greater detail how the church strayed away from the Kingdom message preached by Christ and the disciples/apostles.

So exactly how did the wonderful message of the Kingdom go astray?

The enemy has always been an enemy of the people of Israel for he knows they are God's covenant people. Anti-Semitism (suspicion of, hatred toward, prejudice against Jews alone, because there are other Semitic languages and people) is said to be one of the oldest forms of racism in the world. Jews have suffered persecution in and out of exile for more than 1,000 years. Throughout history, the children of Israel were a hated people: their cultural mindset set them apart from others. Eric Kandel stated that "Jewish-ness" or the "religious or cultural tradition that is acquired through learning...distinctive traditions and education" fueled fears in other cultures of the the Jewish corrupting influence of domination. The Jews considered themselves the covenant people of God and followed the Mosaic Law, which forbade polytheism and intercultural marriage. Additionally, the animal sacrificial system of ancient Judaism was considered crude, and distasteful. You had to be born a Jew to be accepted, or worse yet, one must be educated and religiously converted in order to be accepted in the Jewish society.

During the Intertestamental Period, after the successful Maccabean Revolt, the Jews under Judas Maccabeus, gained their religious freedom (164 BC). Twenty-two years later, they gained political independence and for nearly eight years were ruled by their own leaders, the Hasmonean dynasty of priest-kings. In 63 BC, the Hasmonean kingship ended as Judea fell under Roman control. For a while, Rome governed Judea (called a client kingdom) indirectly through Jewish rulers, such as Herod the Great (37 BC-4 BC). In 6 AD, Judea was given the same kind of two-tiered administration it enjoyed under Persian and Greco-Macedonian rule. The Roman government appointed a provincial governor, called a prefect or procurator, who was responsible for maintaining the peace and arranging the efficient collection of the tributes for Caesar.

For Paul, Rome was the most strategic Gentile location to reach with the gospel. It was the most dominant city in the 1st century. Paul wrote one of his most lengthy theological treatises to the church at Rome, which he desired to reach with the gospel due to its significance to his mission. He understood that if he could impact Rome with the Kingdom message, then it would become a highway for the gospel of the Kingdom to reach the world. As the number of followers of the Christian faith grew, Christians became a persecuted minority, their faith and lifestyle becoming more and more offensive to both the Jews and the Gentiles.

Spawned by Nero, Rome became a city known for Christian persecution. The Emperor Nero, according to the Jewish historian Josephus, had a vision to rebuild Rome according to his image and likeness. He reportedly burned down Rome and blamed it on the Christians, who were an easy scapegoat due to their unconventional religious practices. The Romans wrongly called the Christians "cannibals," believing they were eating Christ's flesh at the Lord's Supper, and accused them of having orgies during their love feasts. Of course, these were nothing more than fellowship meals that included the ordinance of the Lord's Supper. Christians were an easy target, because they did not have the socio-political backing of the Jews or the respect of the Romans.

This persecution was continued by other Roman rulers and was one reason for the Christian Diaspora. It was to persecuted diaspora believers that Peter wrote his epistles with an aim to encourage them in their faith. Persecution continued until 313 AD and was responsible for some of the greatest martyrs of Christendom. Some of those persecuted and executed were the Apostle Paul, Polycarp, Justin Martyr, and a host of others. To discover more about the age of martyrdom, I suggest reading the book entitled, *Foxe's Book of Martyrs* and my book, *The Doors of the Church Are Closed* (www.DrDanaCarson.com).

It is important to note that every act concerning the dispensations of theological renewal, including the cultural hatred for Jews and Christians, and the subsequent persecution and dispersion of Christians, was a part of the providential hand of God. When Constantine the Great signed the Edict of Milan in 313 AD, ending nearly 300 years of Christian persecution (this document allowed all religious expression without persecution), Christians were finally respected and repositioned at the top of all religious classes. How did Constantine come to be the torchbearer for Christianity? It is believed that while facing one of his toughest military battles, the emperor said that he had a vision of Christ, who told him "to mark the heavenly sign of God on the shields of his soldiers." The sign was the Greek letters, *chi* transversed by *rho*, which is represented by an X with a P-like symbol down the middle.

The victory Constantine secured in battle, after applying this symbol on the shields of his soldiers, he attributed to Jesus Christ. It is debatable whether Constantine truly had a vision from God, especially due to some of the changes he would later bring to Christianity. Some scholars doubt whether he ever really had a conversion experience at all; others believe that he gave his life to Christ about 314 AD. Nevertheless, Constantine the Great was responsible for positioning Christianity to be the official religion of the Roman Empire.

Thus, the 4th century was extremely important for Christianity. Negatively, the church transitioned away from the Newer Testament understanding of the Kingdom of God and conformed to the kingdom of this world that embraced it – the Roman Empire. The transition involved the painstaking process of integrating Christianity into the pagan culture of Rome, removing all goals and efforts of establishing the Kingdom of God along the lines of the early church. Rome, during this time, was extremely polytheistic, acknowledging a multiplicity of gods and goddesses and offering all types of sacrifices and offerings to this pantheon of gods. Furthermore, the city was known for sacred festivals, temple priests, and prostitutes. Constantine believed that many pagan beliefs and practices served more to divide and weaken rather than unite the city. Seeing the political advantage of having a one-world religion that could unite the Roman Empire, and having visions of personal political greatness, he conscripted Christianity with its Kingdom-building message for his use to this end. Remember – the message of Christ in the 1st century was the message of God's Kingdom being inaugurated through Jesus Christ and perpetuated by His representatives. But Christ was now dead and had ascended, thus, Constantine, a self-imposed king, provided the structure and the motivation for a Kingdom culture and model of governance.

I believe that Constantine saw in the message of Christ (the Kingdom of God) and the unity of Christianity as a prime opportunity to use religion to empower the structure and infrastructure for a greater Roman Empire. Isn't it interesting that God always has a way to preserve what's important through His hand of providence? So, while Christianity had come through several centuries of mass persecution, hiding in caves and catacombs, it now moved from hidden disgrace to public honor.

Why was Christianity ideal for Rome and Constantine the Great? Because Constantine could see what many contemporary Christians have missed

– the structure and message of the Kingdom of God! He knew that Christianity was not simply about the event of Jesus' death, burial, and resurrection. This great earthly king recognized the one true King—though absent! He knew the life and death of Jesus the Christ was much more than an event – it had created a movement. While Christ's message could be misunderstood as political, Christ was clear that His Kingdom was not of this world. However, the lack of one single compilation of scriptures throughout the Christian churches led to ignorance of the true Kingdom message (different apocryphal Older Testament writings and Newer Testament epistles of the apostles circulated in many Christian communities).

Constantine saw only the political aspect of the Kingdom message and saw it as an opportunity to embrace what the Jews rejected. During this era, a great rift developed between Rome and Judaism. Though the Jews were given religious freedom of expression, embracing Christianity invariably meant the denigration of Judaism for crucifying Jesus Christ. The spirit of anti-Semitism, which already existed, simply deepened and took greater root within the psyche of the Roman Empire and beyond. Rome now embraced what they perceived the Jews rejected, the Lordship of Jesus Christ. Of course, devout and religious Jews had no problem with this, because they had no honor for Christ; they did not consider Him to be the Messiah.

This rift was solidified into law for both the Jews and Roman citizens (who were now Christian), Rome effectively, culturally, and societally separated Christianity from its Jewish roots. Jews were forbidden to own Christian slaves or to circumcise their slaves. Additionally, during the first Council of Nicaea (325 AD), Constantine supported the separation of the celebration of Easter from the Jewish Passover celebration. Clearly anti-Semitic in tone, he stated:

> "...it appeared an unworthy thing that in the celebration of this most holy feast we should follow the practice of the Jews, who have impiously defiled their hands with enormous sin, and are, therefore, deservedly afflicted with blindness of soul... Let us then have nothing in common-

> with the detestable Jewish crowd; for we have received from our Saviour a different way... For we have it in our power, if we abandon their custom, to prolong the due observance of this ordinance to future ages by a truer order."[1]

From that time on, Christians, unlike every century before, ceased to consult with the Jews on when Passover fell according to the Hebrew calendar. The Roman Julian calendar (a solar-based 12 month calendar of 365 days with a leap day added to February every four years), the one we use now, was given precedence over the lunar-based Hebrew calendar.

God allowed and used this period in history to perpetuate and preserve His church. Due to the integration of Christianity into the Roman state, it was decreed and understood that to be a Roman citizen was to be a Christian and to be a Christian was to be a Roman citizen. Constantine essentially established Christianity as an official religion and no longer a sect of Judaism. This mindset led to the practice of infant baptism, which became proof of citizenship and religion. Constantine apparently studied the teachings of Christ and His Kingdom and understood that baptism was connected to regeneration or the new birth and citizenship.

The Kingdom was clearly structured as an empire, but not an empire of this world. Even in that era, there were those who understood that the movement of the Kingdom was not only not relegated to the event of the resurrection, but it also extended into a political movement. Further evidence that the Roman Empire's understanding of the Kingdom of God concerned more than events surrounding Jesus Christ's death, burial, and resurrection was the emergence of monks and monastery. The monks were highly ascetic and believed that Christianity was being made carnal, the spiritual practices and principles being forsaken for political gain. They did not believe that one could go to heaven simply by becoming a Roman citizen and being baptized, but by living out the moral laws of God. Hence, they became extremists and practiced worldly separatism in order to demonstrate what they perceived was the Kingdom lifestyle.

1 Eusebius, *Life of Canstantine Vol. III Ch. XVIII Life of Constantine* (Book III (Catholic Encyclopedia).

The 4th century was plagued by the reality of the clash of the kingdoms. While the non-spiritual focus of the Roman Empire did not perpetuate the essence of the message and mission of the Kingdom of God, it served as a wonderful environment to promote Christianity and the Newer Testament. As a state religion, free from persecution and oppression, the Christian church was able to consolidate its message and solidify its theology. This context provided an opportunity for the church and for Christian leaders to discuss and agree on critical theological positions. The 4th century was when many Christological controversies were addressed and settled.

Many of the patristic fathers such as Athanasius, Augustine, Origen, Tertullian, and others were instrumental in helping to shape Christian doctrine during this time. Through the church councils such as Nicene, Constantinople, Ephesus, Chalcedon, Carthage, and others, the church fathers developed orthodox doctrinal positions on Christ, the Holy Spirit, the Triune nature of God, and compiled the Newer Testament documents. God knew a Kingdom culture could not be perpetuated or internationally disseminated without written literature that contained the values, norms, and mores of the Kingdom society. The Third Council of Carthage in North Africa was an adjutant in this endeavor, finalizing the first canon of the Bible (Older and Newer Testaments) in 397 AD.

While the 4th century was crucial to the theological and structural development of the Christian faith and church, it was spiritually abusive concerning its practices and was also guilty of not obeying the scriptures. The message of Christ and His Kingdom was lifted out of its Jewish context and reshaped and modeled á la the Roman Empire, which adulterated the message of the Kingdom and distorted its vision. Ripped from its Jewish context, the message of Christ and His Kingdom lost its intended meaning. The scriptures declare that He came to His own and they did not receive Him, but to as many as received Him, to them He gave the right to become children of God (John 1:12). The emphasis made is that Jesus came to His own, the Jews, which suggests that we must understand some of the Jewish context of Christ to properly interpret His message. Jesus was a Jew, who came to the Jews first as a part of God's strategic approach to world evangelism. God always intended to reach beyond the Jewish people, not over them, so the Jews' rejection of Christ did not equate to God's rejection of the Jews, nor us. In fact, Paul writes in Romans 9:11 about the necessity of Israel rejecting God in order that the Gentiles be ingrafted into His plan. God began His covenant with the Jews and will end it with the Jews; God always honors His covenant.

The book of Revelation describes how God will ultimately return and redeem His people, the Jews, through rescuing them at the battle of Armageddon.

The lifting of Christ out of His historical Jewish context made it impossible to understand His message, but not His advent. Roman culture infiltrated "the Way" and reshaped its foundations and biblical illuminations. Thus, the church in Rome focused upon His advent and the event of the resurrection, but not His context of the Kingdom. By shifting the focus upon the birth of Christ and the event of His crucifixion and resurrection, they made the Jewish context irrelevant in interpreting scripture. This focus allowed the Kingdom of God to be viewed and understood along the lines of the Roman kingdom.

I reiterate once again – it is impossible to interpret the gospel of the Kingdom outside of its Jewish context. When I was in seminary, I was able to peruse what I thought to be one of the most useful tools I had ever come across. I was introduced to a German biblical commentary set written by Strack and Billerbeck. You may be saying, "Does this man know theological German?" – the answer is absolutely not. The value of this commentary is that you can distinguish the different Newer Testament volumes and then read the Talmudic references at the bottom. This particular commentary set referenced all the Talmudic sources in the gospels.

The Talmud is a commentary on the Mishnah, and the Mishnah is a set of books that contain the oral traditions of the rabbis, designed to add greater levels of difficulties in violating the Law of Moses. Unfortunately, rather than protecting the Law of Moses, it caused the Jews to lose focus of them. My fascination with these commentaries was that whenever the gospels referenced a Jewish practice that was from the Talmud, the name, volume, and section where this law and practice was written in the Talmud was cited. Since I have a copy of the Mishnah and the Talmud, I was able to go to original sources to read the actual oral traditions of the rabbis. Many of the topics and examples Christ used were rooted in Jewish culture, practices, and thought, and in order to contextually understand the message of Christ, you have to be familiar with the Jewish context.

Jesus' culture provided the only context of interpretation of His teachings about the Kingdom of God. The parables and sayings of Jesus cannot be understood outside the Jewish context without changing the message. When you remove the Jewish context, you now remove the ability to accurately interpret and understand His message of the Kingdom. Once one delves into the authentic context of the Christ, you soon discover the context and the content of the good news of the Kingdom that Jesus preached was totally different than the new Roman context under Constantine the Great. The Romanization of the Kingdom movement forever distorted the purity of the gospel of the Kingdom as intended in its Jewish context.

First century Palestine and 4th century Rome had two entirely different societal contexts and worldviews. The Jewish context was a monotheistic one that lifts God above man; the Roman context lifted up the emperor as a god and he told the people whom to serve. Judaism is deeply rooted and grounded in thought and practice as dictated by the Mosaic Law, the prophets, and the Mishnah – the rabbis' attempt to interpret the law.

The Jewish culture was created by a covenant with God through Abraham, Isaac, and Jacob; and the basis of their existence was their belief in one God.

The Romans became a great empire through the hands of their emperors and military generals; the gods, though consulted for guidance, had moderate to minimal influence in the operations of the empire. Jews, on the other hand, were mandated to meet with God during the seven feasts of Israel that were celebrated in three journeys of Passover, Pentecost, and Tabernacles. These feasts are still celebrated in modern Judaism today and are most definitely a part of the Jewish context in which Christ preached the message of the Kingdom. The passion of Christ or His suffering and redemption cannot be fully understood outside of the Jewish context of the feasts. He is the fulfillment of Jewish prophecy and practice. Truly, God's hand ensured that the events of Christ were congruent with the Older Testament Day of Atonement and the events of the Jewish Passover. The trials and testing of Christ were the fulfillment of Yom Kippur or the Day of Atonement. Christ was the unspotted Passover Lamb; and we are Barabbas set free as the scapegoat that was freed. Christ's crucifixion was the sacrifice for the sins of the world; He was the atoning Lamb of God who took away the sins of the world and allowed us access to another Kingdom, the Kingdom of God. This context is so vital to understanding the gospel that it is a travesty to ignore the Jewish roots of Christianity or the Kingdom.

I have always felt a strong need to understand the Jewishness of Christ, because I know that it is key to understanding His message. I'm not a Jewish scholar, but I am a good friend of Dr. Brad Young, the professor of Old Testament and Judaic Studies at a world-class seminary. I have also aligned myself with a Messianic Jewish rabbi, so that I can glean more insight into the Jewish roots and message of Christ. I really desired to study Judaic thought and studies and was accepted into the Brown University doctoral program in Judaic Studies, but could not attend due to the physical requirements of totally relocating. My point is that it is paramount to understand the Jewish context of Christ in order to properly understand His message of the good news of the Kingdom.

One of the greatest events for Christianity also became one of the **MOST DANGEROUS AND DESTRUCTIVE - THE LEGALIZATION OF CHRISTIANITY BY ROME!**

Romanization of the gospel left a huge void in biblical exegesis. You may be saying, "Dr. Carson, is the message that we have been taught invalid?" No, but it is incomplete and not totally accurate. Divine providence is always at work as well as dispensational grace. I believe that the Romanization of the Kingdom of God was a part of the plan of God that would position the church in a place eventually where it could get to a sound biblical understanding of the Kingdom. Romanization was also a tremendous boost for Christianity, because it provided a context for Christian thought due to its appreciation of philosophy and religion. This era produced Christian thinkers who assisted the church in developing some of the most formative and foundational doctrines of the church. However, changing the message of Christ changed the purpose of the church, and scripture is true – without vision, the people cast off restraint (Proverbs 29:18). Abuses in the Christian church, both historically and currently, have provided a foundation for misinterpretation and rejection of the message of Jesus Christ. The Romanization of Christianity was largely responsible for how the world now interprets the Christian faith.

The Vatican is the most powerful religious headquarters in the world and possibly the greatest leader and loudest voice for Christianity worldwide. Its global reach, ecclesiastical structure, political power, economic wealth, and influence over governments have made the Roman Catholic Church a force to be reckoned with historically. This hegemony, along with some of its teachings, has led some to wrongly believe that the Catholic Church is the Kingdom of God. A return to Jesus' Kingdom vision and message will quickly dismiss this claim as bogus. While the Roman Catholic Church was busy being Roman, Christianity's Judaic roots had been severed and its African connection ignored. The only two possible links to the Jewish context of Jesus' message of the Kingdom were forsaken and forgotten.

Coming out of the matrix of Roman Catholicism, Protestantism unfortunately promoted a similar brand of theology and Kingdom perspective, spreading its wings over Europe and colonizing other nations (1500-1900). The Protestant Movement began in Germany – a European country under the holy Roman Empire. One of its priests, a monk and a professor of theology, Martin Luther, was the catalyst for the Protestant Movement.

Martin Luther challenged the theology of the Roman Catholic Church on its view of salvation, which stated that justification depended only on faith that is active in charity and good works (donations to the church). He countered this heresy, posting 95 theses of disputations against this doctrine and arguing for a salvation based on *sola fide, sola gratia, sola scriptura,* and *solus Christus* – "by faith alone, by grace alone, by scripture alone, and by Christ alone is man saved." However, while he understood the original context of Christ was Judaism, he himself was guilty of anti-Semitic thoughts, writings, and practices. Luther never intended to bring down the Roman Catholic Church or address its faulty foundation, only to reform some of its abusive practices against common men.

Martin Luther, nor any of the reformers, fought against the racist, classist, or sexist practices of the Roman Catholic Church. The reformers' focus was upon the doctrine of salvation, which was a very important theme at the time. The Lord's purpose in the reformation prevailed, resulting in the Protestant church today. Because of the work of the reformers and revivalists, the church became aware of doctrinal blind spots and alerted us to be on the lookout for other blind spots. Hence, since the Reformation, God has been preparing the way for the Dispensation of Exaltation – the restoration of the Kingdom of God.

> *Through Roman Catholicism and Protestant colonization, Romanized and Europeanized Christianity has been taught around the globe stemming from the Roman Empire and Constantine the Great.*

So what gospel was preached throughout the 4th century through colonization? Was it the message that Jesus proclaimed in 1st century Galilee and all the villages of its surrounding towns (Matthew 4:23-25; 9:35-38)? Can the message of Christ be properly interpreted without an understanding of the Jewish context that He proclaimed and within which He taught the gospel? The answer to these questions is an overwhelming, "No!" We can understand parts of Christ's message, but not the whole message.

The Roman Catholic Church age did preserve four things of great value to historic Christianity.

1. The deity of Christ
2. The advent of Christ
3. The event of the resurrection referred to as "Easter"
4. The scriptures

The church in the Roman Empire, however, blended in many pagan practices, holidays, and paradigms. The papacy took on a form of apostolic structure, pulling the church out of homes and the fellowship of the people, and placing the celebration of Christ inside public buildings called "basilicas," assigning official religious officers to serve in the church. Because it was a state religion, Christianity became a servant of the empire through the priests, nuns, bishops, cardinals, and pope. However, this order of leadership was not reflective of the Jesus model of Kingdom ministry as taught and practiced in the 1st century. Gone were the five-fold gifts that Jesus Himself placed in the church: apostles, prophets, evangelists, pastors, and teachers (Ephesians 4:11-12). The deleterious effects of these changes can still be felt in the church today!

While Romanization provided an environment that helped to iron out some of the basic doctrines of the Christian faith and theology, while bringing about expansive development to some of the underdeveloped parts of Africa, European colonialist countries attempted to increase their economic strength and wealth under the guise of "expanding God's Kingdom," thereby exploiting the natural and human resources of every country they "discovered" and "converted." The abuses of colonization, oftentimes in the name of God, were devastating to the message of the gospel. Colonialists used the Bible to subjugate, not liberate, as it was written to do, for their own greed. Many indigenous people were forced to give up their culture and embrace Christianity, but were ill-treated in the process by a church that no longer reflected or practiced the values of the true Kingdom of God.

Colonialism was not the breaking in of God's Kingdom on earth. The gospel was used as a supremacist tool to subjugate people in the name of God to a way of life deemed superior, and to promote European culture and values. People were taught more European culture than Bible verses. The colonial traders, businessmen, and religious recruiters were under the impression that the indigenous people of the land lived substandard lives and in order to advance in their existence, they needed to embrace the European culture. People were, therefore, forced to abandon their values and cultures and embrace the so-called 'good news of the European culture' that would make the indigenes better humans; the imperialists in the meantime becoming more and more wealthy as they raped the countries of their natural resources.

> *Pope Benedict XVI said, "The Colonization of the Americas brought* INJUSTICES AND SUFFERINGS TO THE NATIVE PEOPLES, *but it also opened the way to the* PROCLAMATION OF THE GOSPEL *and a unique* "DIALOGUE OF FAITH AND CULTURE."

Colonialism was not the context for the preaching of the gospel of the Kingdom. Actually, it was the establishment of a counter-kingdom. Christ stated that His Kingdom was not of this world (John 18:36). The European culture had been intoxicated by its own heroism. The Roman Empire had convinced itself and the world that Jesus had become European, and He resided in His Kingdom, which was in Rome, within the gates of the Vatican. In fact, today the Vatican has its own country code and is considered to be its own country or kingdom. Jesus' message found no better context in colonialism than Romanization for bearing Kingdom fruit.

The authentic gospel of the Kingdom creates one class of people, a new creation that are characterized as a chosen race, holy nation, a royal priesthood, God's own special people (1 Peter 2:9). The scripture is very clear that in God's Kingdom there is no difference between Jew or Gentile, bondsman or freeman, male or female (Galatians 3:28). But colonialism propagated a gospel of division and distinction. The basis of colonization was racism, classism, and sexism, which are counter-culture to the Kingdom; thus, the good news of the Kingdom was not preached nor understood. You may be asking, "What about those who were sincere about Christ, were they saved? My answer is a resounding "Yes!" I say this for two reasons: 1) They were saved because the advent and event of the resurrection is the basis of salvation and that message was preached in some form, and 2) I believe that God issues dispensational grace, which suggests that God does not hold a person accountable for a truth of which they are ignorant. During colonization, people did not have access to sound biblical truth – only what the colonists taught them, and the colonists themselves were indoctrinated with faulty theology. The basis of the perpetuation of Christianity during these periods was belief in Christ's death, burial, and resurrection. People were embracing Christ as Savior, but really did not understand what it meant for Him to be Lord.

Today's church is not much different. Erroneous teachings and traditions passed down through the years are replete in the church. Modern Christians believe in Jesus Christ, but the culture in which He was born and raised has been successfully minimized (some would say 'sanitized') from His existence. His message has been adulterated. Through Romanization and colonization, Jesus the Christ was kidnapped out of Jewish culture! Can today's church plead ignorance here? No, this culture and this church cannot plead ignorance like the medieval church; we have too much information at our fingertips to remain stuck in tradition. Thus, it is during this day and time that the Kingdom message is being restored, and God is being exalted!

5

Jesus – The Messianic King

By this time, you've repeatedly heard my position on how important Jewish culture is to understanding the Kingdom message of Christ. In this chapter, we will discuss just how significant understanding Jewish culture is in order to properly interpret not only the message of Jesus, but also who Jesus was as the Messiah.

Jesus was born a Jew, lived as a Jew, and died a Jew. He was a descendant of the Semitic Israelites, of the royal lineage of King David. Upon Christ's head was placed a crown of thorns and an inscription – "King of the Jews." If this point is reiterated one million times, it would not be enough for the modern Christian. The authentic background for the message of Christ is not Rome or Europe; it is Palestine; it is Jewish thought, culture, and religious tradition. Jesus was a Jew who practiced the ancient Jewish faith. As my friend and colleague, Dr. Brad Young, states, "Jesus never changed His religion. He recited the Shema and understood its significance like every other Jew."[1]

---

1 Young, Brad. (2007), *Meet the Rabbi*, Peabody, MA: Hendrickson Publisher, pg. 157.

> *"Hear, O Israel: The Lord our God, the Lord is one! You shall love the Lord your God with all your heart, with all your soul, and with all your strength. – Deuteronomy 6:4-5*

Likewise, Jesus' Kingdom mission and ministry only fit within the context of Jewish thought and understanding of the Jewish Messiah.

It cannot be over-emphasized – Jesus was a Jew, lived as a Jew, and died a Jew. Removing Jesus from His Jewish context has not worked and does not work. Remember the movie *Shawshank Redemption*? The movie is about a banker named Andy Dufrense, who serves nearly 20 years in the Shawshank State Prison, where he eventually masterminds his escape. While there, he is assigned to assist elderly inmate Brooks Hatlen in the prison library. When Mr. Hatlen was freed on parole after spending his entire adult life in prison, he tried to live in the free world, but he could not make the adjustment. Eventually, he committed suicide. This is about the closest analogy I could find to describe the ineffectiveness of Jesus outside the Jewish context. Just like Mr. Hatlen, Jesus' identity and His purpose were lost. Jesus was the Messianic King. The concept of the Messiah is important in understanding the ministry of Christ and the gospel of the Kingdom. Jesus was the Messiah; but, He was the Jewish Messiah! For who He was is inextricably connected with the Kingdom of God. So let's talk about the concept of Messiah!

You probably have heard the term "messiah" but don't really have a real understanding of the concept. The birth of Christ was significant in His ministry, for it indicated that He was the Messiah – the long anticipated King of the Jews. The term "messiah" is derived from the Hebrew word *mashiach*, a verbal adjective, which means "anointed one." The Newer Testament or Greek word for "anointed one" is *christos*; *christos* refers to "the act of consecration whereby an individual is set apart for the service of God and anointed (smeared or perhaps sprinkled with oil)." The Jewish ceremonial practice of anointing with oil was very common in the cultural and religious context of Jewish worship and life. Priests were regularly anointed prior to their divinely appointed service at the altar of sacrifice:

> *...if the anointed priest sins, bringing guilt on the people, then let him offer to the Lord for his sin which he has sinned a young bull without blemish as a sin offering. – Leviticus 4:3*

The anointing of Hebrew (synonymous with Jewish) kings with balsam was also a common practice in Israel. However, there is no strong scriptural support for the anointing of a prophet.

Samuel established the act and prerequisite of being anointed prior to royal service in Israel by anointing Saul (1 Samuel 10:1) the first king of Israel (also David – 2 Samuel 2:4, Jehu – 2 Kings 9:6, and Joash – 2 Kings 11:12). The king, in Jewish thought, was thought to be the Lord's anointed man and held a secure position before men. The Jewish people, based upon royal protocol and practice, expected a great king according to Messianic prophecies that spoke of an anointed one who would come and bring salvation to Israel. The prophetic expectation of the Messiah coming to restore Israel back to religious and political power was so prevalent in the Jewish mind that the 13 articles of Hebraic faith, which we attribute to Moses Maimonides (a rabbi, not the Moses of the Bible) in the 13th century, refers to the coming Messiah. The 13 principles of faith are printed in every Jewish prayer book and are recited as a liturgical hymn at the conclusion of a Friday or Festival Service.[2] These principles are recited during the synagogue service and are known as the Yigdal, which means "Let God be exalted." The 13 principles of the Jewish faith are similar to Christian creeds; they are the embodiment of Judaism's fundamental and traditional pillars and beliefs.

Maimonides' 12th principle in the Jewish articles of faith affirms the future coming of the Messiah. Modern day Jews state in their prayer Hebrew books, "I believe with a perfect heart that the Messiah will come; and although His coming be delayed, I will still wait patiently for His speedy appearance."[3] This is also a Christian belief; however, the difference is that orthodox Jews see the coming of the Messiah as His first arrival. Christians, on the other hand, believe that the Messiah has already come

---

2 Ibid.

3 Walter A. Elwell, Ph.D., Philip W. Comfort, Ph.D., *Tyndale Bible Dictionary*, Tyndale House Publishers, Inc., p. 887.

in the person of Jesus of Nazareth. Both Jews and Christians embrace the concept of God's anointed one coming to establish His Kingdom. For us, though, Jesus is the anointed of God. His anointing was consistent with the Older Testament anointings of the office of the priest and king. Jesus was anointed as the great High Priest who could enter the veil, and He was anointed as the King of Israel. Thus, an understanding of the Jewish Messiah is critical to understanding the essence of the gospel of the Kingdom.

The coming of the Messiah was the hope of Israel, a Jewish expectation that would have worldwide implications. In Jewish thought (Mishnah) and understanding, at His coming, the Messiah would usher in an era of peace; there would be no war, no hunger, no envy, no competition – basic goodness and decency would permeate the world and influence all men toward good. It was understood that no man knew the day or the hour of the coming of the Messiah, but was instructed to patiently wait upon Him. The Jewish hope for the advent of the Messiah is reflected in the prophetic utterance of the Prophet Nathan that the reign of David would endure to the end of time:

> *"When your days are fulfilled and you rest with your fathers, I will set up your seed after you, who will come from your body, and I will establish his Kingdom. He shall build a house for My name, and I will establish the throne of his Kingdom forever. I will be his Father, and he shall be My son. If he commits iniquity, I will chasten him with the rod of men and with the blows of the sons of men. But My mercy shall not depart from him, as I took it from Saul, whom I removed from before you. And your house and your Kingdom shall be established forever before you. Your throne shall be established forever." ' " According to all these words and according to all this vision, so Nathan spoke to David. – 2 Samuel 7:12-17*

Israel was told, through the prophetic voice, that David's throne would be perpetuated through his descendants and his throne would have a never-ending dominion over all the earth (2 Samuel 22:48-51). Jeremiah the prophet also spoke prophetically of the throne of David and its connection to Christ:

'Behold, the days are coming,' says the Lord, 'that I will perform that good thing which I have promised to the house of Israel and to the house of Judah:

'In those days and at that time
I will cause to grow up to David
A Branch of righteousness;
He shall execute judgment and righteousness in the earth.
In those days Judah will be saved,
And Jerusalem will dwell safely.
And this is the name by which she will be called:

THE LORD OUR RIGHTEOUSNESS.'

"For thus says the Lord: 'David shall never lack a man to sit on the throne of the house of Israel; nor shall the priests, the Levites, lack a man to offer burnt offerings before Me, to kindle grain offerings, and to sacrifice continually.'" – Jeremiah 33:14-18

The Messianic age and expectation dominated the mindset of the Jewish people. This hope was nurtured even when over 200 years had passed following the death of King Solomon, and even when the truncated northern kingdom of Israel was assimilated into the Assyrian homelands and the house of David seemed to be nearing annihilation. Even though Israel had a spotty history of apostate kings that culminated with the Babylonian rule and exile, they still maintained a faith in the coming of the Messiah. During the final three centuries before Christ, a flourishing community at Qumran lived in expectation of the coming One's advent. They anticipated their own charismatic figure, which they referred to as "the Teacher of Righteousness and the Expounder of the law." The pseudepigraphal book of Jubilees chapter 23, written around 100 BC, cites that God Himself will usher in the age to come, which is referred to as the Golden Age. This Golden Age will overturn the evils of Satan, who is the ruler of a counter-kingdom of evil. In the Golden Age, good will triumph over evil, bringing healing and the expulsion of demons. When Jesus came, He used this concept to explain the Kingdom.

He answered and said to them: "He who sows the good seed is the Son of Man. The field is the world, the good seeds are the sons of the kingdom, but the tares are the sons of the wicked one. The enemy who sowed them is the devil, the harvest is the end of the age, and the reapers are the angels. Therefore as the tares are gathered and burned in the fire, so it will be at the end of this age. The Son of Man will send out His angels, and they will gather out of His kingdom all things that offend, and those who practice lawlessness, and will cast them into the furnace of fire. There will be wailing and gnashing of teeth. Then the righteous will shine forth as the sun in the kingdom of their Father. He who has ears to hear, let him hear! – Matthew 13:37-43

Later, the Jewish rabbis taught the coming of the Messiah with detail. Preoccupation with the Messiah is evident in the tractate Sanhedrin (Babylonian Talmud) where passages state that the world was created for Him and that all the prophets prophesied of His days (Sanhedrin 98b, 99a). The rabbis applied no fewer than 456 passages of scripture to His Person and salvation. By and large, orthodoxy still retains its time-worn belief in the Messiah's reign in Jerusalem, the rebuilding of the great Temple, and the re-establishment of both priesthood and sacrifice. The coming of the Jewish Messiah was the preoccupation of every Jew, including the disciples and Paul. The disciples were so consumed by the Messianic promise that after the resurrection of Christ, they expected a restoration of the throne of David and the establishment of the Kingdom of God in their social and political lives. Some believed that perhaps Judas, who was a zealot, did not intend for Christ to be crucified, which is evident by his suicide. It is believed that he became impatient with the lack of political advancement toward the Kingdom and tried to precipitate it by forcing Jesus' hand to bring it about. After all, he was convinced by what he experienced and saw that Jesus was the prophesied Messiah. Judas wanted Him to restore the Kingdom right here on earth and right then. However, it did not go his way, but according to the will of God. All the disciples wanted the same thing – the restoration of the political kingdom of Israel that would liberate them from the rule of the Roman Empire. Thus, Luke writes:

> *Therefore, when they had come together, they asked Him, saying, "Lord, will You at this time restore the kingdom to Israel?" And He said to them, "It is not for you to know times or seasons which the Father has put in His own authority. – Acts 1:6-7*

The disciples' question about the restoration of the Kingdom was full proof that they knew that Jesus was the Messiah who was prophesied of in the Hebrew scriptures; now they wanted Him to simply take the necessary actions and place them in their rightful place in the Kingdom.

The gospel of Matthew outlines a detailed genealogy of Jesus in order to establish His royal lineage from King David and thus, establish Him as the Messiah. To the average modern Christian's eye, this list of ancestors is similar to the other genealogical lists in the Older Testament, but to most, the names have no meaning and the list has no meaning. However, to the Jewish reader of Matthew's gospel account, this list is monumental:

> *The book of the genealogy of Jesus Christ, the Son of David, the Son of Abraham: Abraham begot Isaac, Isaac begot Jacob, and Jacob begot Judah and his brothers. Judah begot Perez and Zerah by Tamar, Perez begot Hezron, and Hezron begot Ram. Ram begot Amminadab, Amminadab begot Nahshon, and Nahshon begot Salmon. Salmon begot Boaz by Rahab, Boaz begot Obed by Ruth, Obed begot Jesse, and Jesse begot David the king. David the king begot Solomon by her who had been the wife of Uriah. Solomon begot Rehoboam, Rehoboam begot Abijah, and Abijah begot Asa. Asa begot Jehoshaphat, Jehoshaphat begot Joram, and Joram begot Uzziah. Uzziah begot Jotham, Jotham begot Ahaz, and Ahaz begot Hezekiah.Hezekiah begot Manasseh, Manasseh begot Amon, and Amon begot Josiah. Josiah begot Jeconiah and his brothers about the time they were carried away to Babylon. And after they were brought to Babylon, Jeconiah begot Shealtiel, and Shealtiel begot Zerubbabel. Zerubbabel begot Abiud, Abiud begot Eliakim, and Eliakim begot Azor. Azor begot Zadok, Zadok begot Achim, and Achim begot Eliud. Eliud begot Eleazar, Eleazar begot Matthan, and Matthan begot Jacob. And Jacob begot Joseph the husband of Mary, of whom was born Jesus who is called Christ. So all the generations from Abraham to David are fourteen generations, from*

> *David until the captivity in Babylon are fourteen generations, and from the captivity in Babylon until the Christ are fourteen generations. – Matthew 1:1-17*

Matthew is intentional in connecting Jesus the man to the lineage of David. Luke also ensures that Jesus is acknowledged as the Messiah:

> *Then the angel said to her, "Do not be afraid, Mary, for you have found favor with God. And behold, you will conceive in your womb and bring forth a Son, and shall call His name Jesus. He will be great, and will be called the Son of the Highest; and the Lord God will give Him the throne of His father David. And He will reign over the house of Jacob forever, and of His kingdom there will be no end." – Luke 1:30-33*

> *Joseph also went up from Galilee, out of the city of Nazareth, into Judea, to the city of David, which is called Bethlehem, because he was of the house and lineage of David, to be registered with Mary, his betrothed wife, who was with child. So it was, that while they were there, the days were completed for her to be delivered. And she brought forth her firstborn Son, and wrapped Him in swaddling cloths, and laid Him in a manger, because there was no room for them in the inn. – Luke 2:4-7*

Both of these gospel writers were inspired by the Holy Spirit to write, so the fact that they wrote in specific detail linking Christ to the city of David, the throne of David, and the lineage of David is providential. The prophets, Isaiah and Micah, wrote of the coming of the Messiah and that He would sit upon the throne of David and have a government that would have no end:

> *Therefore, the Lord Himself will give you a sign: Behold, the virgin shall conceive and bear a Son, and shall call His name Immanuel. Curds and honey He shall eat, that He may know to refuse the evil and choose the good. For before the Child shall know to refuse the evil and choose the good, the land that you dread will be forsaken by both her kings. – Isaiah 7:14-16*

For unto us a Child is born,
Unto us a Son is given;
And the government will be upon His shoulder.
And His name will be called
Wonderful, Counselor, Mighty God,
Everlasting Father, Prince of Peace.
Of the increase of His government and peace
There will be no end,
Upon the throne of David and over His kingdom,
To order it and establish it with judgment and justice
From that time forward, even forever.
The zeal of the Lord of hosts will perform this. – Isaiah 9:6-7

"But you, Bethlehem Ephrathah,
Though you are little among the thousands of Judah,
Yet out of you shall come forth to Me
The One to be Ruler in Israel,
Whose goings forth are from of old,
From everlasting."
Therefore He shall give them up,
Until the time that she who is in labor has given birth;
Then the remnant of His brethren
Shall return to the children of Israel.
And He shall stand and feed His flock
In the strength of the Lord,
In the majesty of the name of the Lord His God;
And they shall abide,
For now He shall be great
To the ends of the earth;
And this One shall be peace. – Micah 5:2-5

Jesus was the fulfillment of these prophecies as recorded in the gospel according to Matthew:

Now the birth of Jesus Christ was as follows: After His mother Mary was betrothed to Joseph, before they came together, she was found with child of the Holy Spirit. Then Joseph her husband, being a just man, and not wanting to make her a public example, was minded to put her away secretly. But while he thought about these things, behold, an angel of the Lord appeared to him in a dream, saying, "Joseph, son of David, do not be afraid to take to you Mary your wife, for that which is conceived in her is of the Holy Spirit. And she will bring forth a Son, and you shall call His name Jesus, for He will save His people from their sins." So all this was done that it might be fulfilled which was spoken by the Lord through the prophet, saying: "Behold, the virgin shall be with child, and bear a Son, and they shall call His name Immanuel," which is translated, "God with us." Then Joseph, being aroused from sleep, did as the angel of the Lord commanded him and took to him his wife, and did not know her till she had brought forth her firstborn Son. And he called His name Jesus. – Matthew 1:18-25

The fact that Jesus is the Messiah, which is rooted in a Kingdom context, allows us to understand the utmost importance of understanding the Kingdom in a Jewish context. I believe in order to have a deeper understanding and appreciation for the gospel of the Kingdom, which Jesus preached, we must understand a little of the context in which He preached and practiced it.

Jesus was the King and came to make known the dispensation of the Kingdom. When you and I read the Bible, this is foreign to us – the Kingdom cultural norms and practices. So we, immediately and subconsciously, interpret the texts within the context that we live and through the things we experience. Unfortunately, this method, though expeditious for relevant application, causes us to interpret the scripture out of its context and thus misunderstand what it means. Interpreting scripture that way, we miss the underlying message and read into the text something we bring to it, an interpretive method called "eisegesis." Instead, our task when we read scripture is one of exegesis whereby we bring or pull out the intended meaning cradled in the text. For example, in the birth of Jesus, it records that there was no room in the inn. Immediately, the modern Western reader thinks about our contemporary context of hotels, motels, Holiday Inn, etc., but this was not the case in the birth narrative. There were no public hostels for travelers in Bethlehem and, if there were, they certainly did not exist the way you and I imagine them. Most of the housing in Bethlehem was cut out of caves and constructed as a two to three-space sized lodgings. Many residences, where the lower class people lived, were simply one large space with a dividing fence; the animals were placed on one side and the people lodged on the other. In the case of the birth of Christ, it simply meant that there were no human accommodations available for Him; He probably was born in the animal space or where the animals fed (an eating trough).

It is **IMPORTANT** *to try to* **UNDERSTAND THE CONTEXT OF SCRIPTURE** *as much as possible, because it can make the* **DIFFERENCE BETWEEN TRUTH AND HERESY.**

When we read the scripture through the lens of our contemporary culture and context, we may misinterpret the life of Christ because we bypass the original context. However, we must see Christ as the 1st century Jews saw Him, and we must understand His message through that cultural medium before contemporizing it.

In today's church, the Bible is simply viewed as a book of rules and regulations, but the Bible contains the precious revelation of God in Christ the King and the coming of His Kingdom. In rabbinical literature, the glory of the King is truth, therefore His Word must be irrevocable (Ta'an. 32a, B.B. 3b). The Bible reveals the great plan and execution of the redemption of humanity that will embrace Him as Lord and Savior. It is a book of covenant that teaches you how to maximize your walk with God as you execute the vision of God for your life as a Kingdom citizen. It is sad to realize that the contemporary church has grown so lukewarm that it doesn't even aspire to know truth any longer. We must study the Word so that we do not fall prey to deception. The Bible instructs and warns us to stay active in our study:

> *Be diligent to present yourself approved to God, a worker who does not need to be ashamed, rightly dividing the word of truth. – 2 Timothy 2:15*

...that we should no longer be children, tossed to and fro and carried about with every wind of doctrine, by the trickery of men, in the cunning craftiness of deceitful plotting, but, speaking the truth in love, may grow up in all things into Him who is the head—Christ... – Ephesians 4:14-15

Then Jesus said to those Jews who believed Him, "If you abide in My word, you are My disciples indeed. 32 And you shall know the truth, and the truth shall make you free." – John 8:31-32

Take heed to yourself and to the doctrine. Continue in them, for in doing this you will save both yourself and those who hear you. – 1 Timothy 4:16

And they continued steadfastly in the apostles' doctrine and fellowship, in the breaking of bread, and in prayers. – Acts 2:42

God's appeal to "seek first the Kingdom..." is only effective to those who have sensitivity to His Word. Today's Christians have learned how to be Christians without the Bible; they have learned how to travel without the Way. Being a Christian without the Bible is like being a lawyer practicing law without the proper source and guide, or a doctor without knowledge of medicine drawn from medical resource. It is impossible to pass the board examination without having studied these disciplines, and so it is impossible to pass the judgment of God without studying the Word of God! However, now is the time for the church to study the Bible, exegeting its wisdom, and interpreting the message through a Jewish contextual prism.

From the time of His announcement, birth, childhood, adulthood, and death, the Jews and others recognized Christ as King. Granted – not everyone appreciated His Kingship, but it was clear that Christ was born King of the Jews. As mentioned earlier, His birth was connected to the throne of David. The wise men were seeking Him who was to be born King of the Jews; the angels announced that the Savior would be born in the City of David – Bethlehem. It is clear that Jesus was the Messianic King; the wise men gave the young baby gifts of gold, frankincense, and myrrh. These were gifts symbolizing His Kingship and death as the Passover Lamb. Thus, they recognized Jesus as Lord and Savior by the gifts that they brought. Not only did the wise men present royal gifts to the young child, Jesus, signifying His Kingship, but there were other Jewish events that happened in the life of Christ that also pointed to His Kingship. But you have to be Jewish or study Judaism to recognize them. Mary anointing Jesus' feet with oil was also an acknowledgment of His Kingship. The Bible references many instances where perfumed oil was used, in particular for kings and to prepare the body for death; the Greek word for "oil" used in this scripture, *muron*, is the same word used to describe one of the gifts given by the wise men – what we know as myrrh (Matthew 2:11). Christ recognized her discernment and stated that her action would be a memorial for her:

> *And when Jesus was in Bethany at the house of Simon the leper, a woman came to Him having an alabaster flask of very costly fragrant oil, and she poured it on His head as He sat at the table. But when His disciples saw it, they were indignant, saying, "Why this waste? For this fragrant oil might have been sold for much and given to the poor." But when Jesus was aware of it, He said to them, "Why do you trouble the woman? For she has done a good work for Me. For you have the poor with you always, but Me you do not have always. For in pouring this fragrant oil on My body, she did it for My burial. Assuredly, I say to you, wherever this gospel is preached in the whole world, what this woman has done will also be told as a memorial to her." – Matthew 26:6-13*

Another cultural event that we just read over, not understanding the context, occurred on what we celebrate as Palm Sunday.

> *Now when they drew near Jerusalem, and came to Bethphage, at the Mount of Olives, then Jesus sent two disciples, saying to them, "Go into the village opposite you, and immediately you will find a donkey tied, and a colt with her. Loose them and bring them to Me. And if anyone says anything to you, you shall say, 'The Lord has need of them,' and immediately he will send them." All this was done that it might be fulfilled which was spoken by the prophet, saying:*

"Tell the daughter of Zion,
'Behold, your King is coming to you,
Lowly, and sitting on a donkey,
A colt, the foal of a donkey.' "

So the disciples went and did as Jesus commanded them. They brought the donkey and the colt, laid their clothes on them, and set Him on them. And a very great multitude spread their clothes on the road; others cut down branches from the trees and spread them on the road. Then the multitudes who went before and those who followed cried out, saying:

"Hosanna to the Son of David!
'Blessed is He who comes in the name of the Lord!'
Hosanna in the highest!"
And when He had come into Jerusalem, all the city was moved, saying, "Who is this?" So the multitudes said, "This is Jesus, the prophet from Nazareth of Galilee." – Matthew 21:1-11

The Prophet Zechariah (9:9) prophesied that the Messiah would come riding on a donkey. In 21st century thought, we would look at a grown man riding a donkey with a smirk due to our cultural ignorance. We prize the horse; no one in our contemporary society looks at a mule with honor. It could never enter the Kentucky Derby and wear a wreath. We see a donkey as a lowly beast of burden, not an animal of honor. However, in the biblical and Jewish context, mules were chiefly members of the royal court and were ridden by kings. King David rode a mule, and Solomon rode to his anointing on King David's mule. The mule that Jesus rode was a young colt and had never been ridden on, which signified His divine Kingship. Thus, riding on the donkey into Jerusalem was a Messianic sign.

You love righteousness and hate wickedness;
Therefore God, Your God, has anointed You
With the oil of gladness more than Your companions.
All Your garments are scented with myrrh and aloes and cassia,
Out of the ivory palaces, by which they have made You glad. – Psalm 45:7-8

Who is this coming out of the wilderness
Like pillars of smoke,
Perfumed with myrrh and frankincense,
With all the merchant's fragrant powders?
Behold, it is Solomon's couch,
With sixty valiant men around it,
Of the valiant of Israel. – Song of Solomon 3:6-7

When we read these passages of scripture, they give us some Jewish insights that help us understand some of the context of Jesus the Messiah. He had just been anointed with expensive perfumed oil, the kind of fragrance with which a king is anointed. The king was known for a sweet smelling aroma, as the above scriptures suggest. Mary anointed Jesus with royal fragrances, and the next week He paraded on a mule into Jerusalem. His vehicle for transportation and the smells, which followed Him, clearly signaled the context and behavior of a king. Consider this text, and compare it to Christ coming on a mule:

So Zadok the priest, Nathan the prophet, Benaiah the son of Jehoiada, the Cherethites, and the Pelethites went down and had Solomon ride on King David's mule, and took him to Gihon. Then Zadok the priest took a horn of oil from the tabernacle and anointed Solomon. And they blew the horn, and all the people said, "Long live King Solomon!" And all the people went up after him; and the people played the flutes and rejoiced with great joy, so that the earth seemed to split with their sound. – 1 Kings 1:38-40

Is this not reminiscent of the coronation of Christ, as the people cried, "Hosanna," which means "Save us?" It is clear that the text is filled with Messianic overtones from the shouting of the children to the waving of the branches. With the lingering effects of the fragrances from the anointing of Mary, Christ, in his last days on earth, more than likely carried a sweet-smelling scent – the scent of a king! From Gethsemane to the cross, Christ carried the scent of a king – what a message God sent to those who arrested Him, accused Him, beat Him, and sentenced Him! Even from the cross, there hung a sign in multiple languages – King of the Jews! He was born a King and died a King; He was and is the Messiah, the anointed one of God. Though the Sadducees and other Jewish religious leaders did not want Pilate to put King of the Jews on His placard (they wanted the sign to say He claimed to be King of the Jews), Pilate wanted to send a strong message to the Jewish religious leaders. In the mind of Roman leadership, they had crucified the King of the Jews, and that sign was a strong warning and statement of the strength of Rome and the weakness of Jews concerning their future deliverance from the power of the Roman Empire. Jesus is *Yeshua Hammashiach* – JESUS THE MESSIAH!

THE GOSPEL OF THE KINGDOM *was preached by* **THE KING OF THE KINGDOM** *who God sent to* **PROCLAIM THE KINGDOM, EXPLAIN THE KINGDOM, AND DEMONSTRATE THE KINGDOM** *as the redemptive atoning Passover Lamb of God.*

The Messiahship of Jesus is clearly proclaimed in all four gospels. In Acts, Peter at Pentecost affirmed this fact (2:36), and Philip to the Ethiopian eunuch (Acts 2:36; 8:32-35). When Peter declared that He had been made both Lord and Christ, Peter was affirming that the resurrection confirmed Christ (Acts 2:36) as the Messiah. Paul declared in the epistle to the Romans that Christ was the Messiah and His resurrection confirmed it (Romans 1:4). He declared his call to the gospel of God, and Christ as the Messianic fulfillment of the prophets, which was confirmed through the power of the resurrection from the dead.

> *Paul, a bondservant of Jesus Christ, called to be an apostle, separated to the gospel of God which He promised before through His prophets in the Holy Scriptures, concerning His Son Jesus Christ our Lord, who was born of the seed of David according to the flesh, and declared to be the Son of God with power according to the Spirit of holiness, by the resurrection from the dead. Through Him we have received grace and apostleship for obedience to the faith among all nations for His name, among whom you also are the called of Jesus Christ... – Romans 1:1-6*

Paul used the resurrection as a patent of declaration to Jesus' right to the title of Messiah. For Paul, Christ was at the very core of his preaching and nothing was/is worthy to be compared to the glory of the Messiah (Philippians 3:5-10).

In the Jewish culture, everyone was aware of what and who Jesus was and what His disciples purported Him to be. That is why Jesus could not simply be ignored and was the reason why early Christians were persecuted by both the Jews and the Romans – they were worshiping a King other than Caesar or Herod. This was dynamite waiting to explode in a revolution against Rome. Modern Christians must also come to "know" the One in whom they believe – Jesus the Messianic King!

> "The personal realization of the Messiah's true identity is not the achievement of personal study and reflection; it is the result of a loving God taking the initiative to reveal Himself to the hearts of those He Himself has prepared to receive the person of His Son, the Lamb as well as the Lion of the tribe of Judah.[4]

---

4 Elwell, W. A., & Beitzel, B. J. (1988), *Baker Encyclopedia of the Bible* (1447–1449), Grand Rapids, MI: Baker Book House.

6

The Gospel of the Kingdom, the Early Church, and the Apostle Paul

The inauguration of the Kingdom was highly anticipated and divinely appointed for a particular time and season. The Hebrew scriptures prophesied of the Messiah and the Intertestamental Period caused the Jewish people to understand this King in apocalyptic terms. And of course, Jesus inaugurated the Kingdom; He began His ministry preaching and teaching the gospel of the Kingdom or the good news of the Kingdom (Matthew 4:23), but He was not alone. At the end of the Intertestamental Period, the scripture records a herald that spoke about the Kingdom of God. His name was John the baptizing one. Speaking of John in Matthew 11, Jesus told the multitude that John was more than a prophet – he was also the fulfillment of prophecy as the messenger who came to prepare the way (Malachi 3:1). He proclaimed, "The Kingdom of God is at hand" (Matthew 3:2). He prepared the people in a form of cleansing and repentance (water baptism) in order to prepare their hearts for the One who would baptize with fire. His message was simply "The Kingdom is coming; it is near; are you ready?" Later, after the death of Christ, His disciples and others preached the message of the Kingdom. The gospels teach us that Christ came preaching the Kingdom of God (in Matthew – the Kingdom of heaven). So, in essence, through writings, they also proclaimed the message of the Kingdom. Many of the Newer Testament writings were compiled and passed around the churches in Palestine and abroad, and the Kingdom of God expanded.

Mark and Luke were not a part of the original 12 disciples; it is believed that Mark was a disciple of Peter, and Luke was a companion of Paul. Yet, their accounts of the life and message of Jesus and the Kingdom of God sometimes use the same wording and the same sequence. Scholars have attempted to understand how the synoptic (seen together) gospels were formed. Some believe Mark was the first document in use, others Matthew, others Luke or John. However, the congruence of the narratives and the message indicate the inspirational hand of God. The author of the gospel of John, who was also an original disciple of Jesus and wrote three epistles (1, 2, and 3 John) and the book of Revelation, also reflects his extensive knowledge of the Greeks and their philosophical beliefs. All four of the gospels, the synoptics and John, record that the focus of Christ's ministry and message was the breaking in of God's Kingdom.

The focus of the gospels is the gospel of the Kingdom. Though not as explicit, it was also the theme of Paul's preaching—and, arguably, of the other apostles' as well. The early church embraced and preached the Kingdom of God. Jesus' words to the disciples were: "And this gospel of the kingdom will be preached in the whole world as a testimony to all nations, and then the end will come" (Matthew 24:14). Would the apostles and the early church invent some other message? No! The Kingdom message was at the heart of all the early church preached.

The book of Acts (also written by the gospel writer Luke) opens with the disciples concerned about the restoration of the Kingdom back to Israel. Christ's message of the Kingdom was so strikingly resonant and clear that the disciples understood it as a political, economic Kingdom. However,

Christ illumined their minds and expanded their vision to include a global focus. When you examine the practices of the early church, as recorded in the book of Acts, it is clear that the early church did not only preach the advent and the event of the resurrection. The early believers saw themselves as the property, slaves, servants, and vessels of God to be used for the Kingdom. They continued to meet in the Temple, and went from house to house sharing the Kingdom message. This was an indication that they did not see Christ as disassociating Himself from His Jewish roots, but fulfilling them. Christ did not come to condemn the Jews nor the world, but to save them. However, the Bible states that He came to His own, and His own received Him not (John 1:11-12). Christ most definitely came to fulfill Jewish prophecy, but also to fulfill the global vision that God had given to Abram. God told Abram that in him all the nations of the world would be blessed (Genesis 12:2-3).

During the Newer Testament era, citizenship was everything and granted one certain rights and privileges. It was an indicator of a person's social value and stature. Jesus' disciples initially saw Kingdom citizenship as a symbol of national, political, and economic status (Acts 1:6-8). So when Christ came preaching that citizenship in heaven is available, it was revolutionary. It is instructive that for 40 days after His resurrection, Jesus spoke to his disciples about the Kingdom. And in His last meeting with them, that was the theme. That session might have been a refresher, a summation of the main things He wanted them to remember. There can be no Kingdom without citizens, however, with citizenship come rights and privileges. That was how Jesus' disciples understood it. James and John wanted a place of honor, power, and privilege in that Kingdom (Mark 10:35-37)—and so did the other disciples. At the last meeting in the upper room, the disciples interpreted Jesus' parting promise of the Holy Spirit as the necessary power to rule in the Kingdom (Acts 1:4-6). And it was—but not the political power the disciples were expecting. It was spiritual power for service in a spiritual Kingdom.

Not until after Pentecost would the disciples and the emerging church understand the Kingdom of God as the spiritual reign of God to which they and all who believe in Jesus belong. Through an examination of the Newer

Testament epistles and the book of Acts, it is clear that Christ intended for those who have a relationship with Him to press themselves into the Kingdom.

The early church saw themselves as Kingdom citizens, representatives of God's Kingdom, not simply church members. Acts 2 begins by placing the new community of Kingdom citizens under a new leadership structure. Apparently, there was a respect for the Jewish religious order, because they went to the Temple daily. But God placed this new covenant people, Kingdom citizens, under a new Kingdom government. The Bible states that they submitted themselves to the apostles' teachings or doctrine (Acts 2:42; 4:32), and under apostolic leadership, they had a unified vision and shared resources. This new community of citizens was a giving people, growing people, grace-filled people, and fellowshiping people. They gave their hearts to Christ and became citizens of His Kingdom, abandoning the kingdom of Satan. They understood who they were in light of Christ, who had changed their lives completely. They lived and existed to expand the message of the Kingdom. Throughout the book of Acts, it is clear that the apostles and others whom the Lord called were inundated with spreading the good news of the Kingdom. The gospels teach us what Christ taught and the book of Acts records the fulfillment of those teachings.

You may ask why the early church focused upon the Kingdom. Before His ascension, the disciples asked Jesus if that was the time the Kingdom would be restored to Israel. They were focused on the Kingdom; however, they did not understand the depth and width of the Kingdom of God. Jesus told the 11 gathered disciples and others to gather in Jerusalem in order to be endued with power so that they would become witnesses of Him first in Jerusalem, then Judea, Samaria, and the end of the earth (Acts 1:8). With those words, they watched Him ascend in a cloud. In obedience to the King, 120 disciples gathered in the upper room for the Feast of Weeks (most commonly known as Pentecost) and waited for the power of the Holy Spirit in order to do Kingdom business.

In chapter 2 of the book of Acts, the Holy Spirit descended as Jesus said He would. Divided tongues sat upon the heads of the 120 waiting believers, and they began to speak in tongues as the evidence. With power from on high, Peter emerged from among them and preached his first message, exhorting the people:

> *"Therefore let all the house of Israel know assuredly that God has made this Jesus, whom you crucified, both Lord and Christ." – Acts 2:36*

Luke does not record the full message of Peter. What we have in Acts 2 does not mention the word "kingdom." However, this should not be understood to mean that his message has no hint of it. By making Christ Lord and Christ after the resurrection, God had elevated Jesus Christ as King over the Kingdom He had come to establish, and all who come under the reign of this King and become Kingdom citizens must acknowledge Christ as their only King, Savior, and Lord. The hearers, pricked in their heart by the Holy Spirit, asked what they needed to do to enter the Kingdom of God, and Peter told them to repent and be saved from this perverse generation (Acts 2:37-38, 40). On the day of Pentecost, the second of the three festivals that required travel and the attendance of the Jews, the first harvest of the spiritual feast occurred – 3,000 souls were added to the church.

The early church did not abandon the message of Christ and turn to their own version of the gospel of the Kingdom. What has to be clear is that they were simply obeying and teaching what they had been taught by the apostles about the Kingdom and what had been fulfilled in Jesus the Messiah. With the message of the Kingdom, they demonstrated the agenda of the Kingdom, and the book of Acts describes how the Kingdom message spread from Judea to the uttermost parts of the world. The message of the Kingdom that began in Jerusalem had spread to Samaria by way of persecution led by Saul of Tarsus. A revival broke out. What was the message, or the gospel, that spread to Samaria and served as the foundation for revival? It was the preaching of the Kingdom by Deacon Phillip:

> *But when they believed Philip as he preached the things concerning the kingdom of God and the name of Jesus Christ, both men and women were baptized. Then Simon himself also believed; and*

when he was baptized he continued with Philip, and was amazed, seeing the miracles and signs which were done. – Acts 8:12-13

Philip proclaimed the Kingdom, explained the Kingdom, and demonstrated its presence with miraculous signs and wonders.

What was the message Paul preached, and did it contradict the message of Jesus in the gospels? The answer is "No." Paul proclaimed the death, burial, and resurrection of Jesus. These events were crucial to the enthronement of Christ as Lord and King, a theme that threads through Peter's Pentecost sermon and much of Acts – Jesus who died to save our lives so that He can be Lord of our lives. That is what His death, resurrection, and exaltation signify. It is not enough to confess Jesus as Savior; we must come under His rule and lordship. It is erroneous to see Paul or the other apostles teaching a gospel antithetical to what Christ taught, rather than what they taught flowing out of what Christ taught. The apostles did not have *carte blanche* in sermon and teaching selections. As Christ declared only what He heard the Father saying and only did what He saw the Father doing (John 5:19), so the apostles' words and deeds reflected Christ's. I hope you are catching this in your spirit man, because God is trying to communicate to the church through the context He sovereignly chose.

Understanding Kingdom

You and I live in a democratic republic, and do not have a clue of what it's like living in a kingdom. Even the contemporary kingdoms that exist today are nothing like the ancient kingdoms whose character and function frame scripture. So we are at a disadvantage and run the risk of misunderstanding the Newer Testament concept of Kingdom. For example, the British kingdom, which often comes to mind to the Western person, is a flawed model of God's Kingdom.

Historically, kings normally came to power by appointment or were made kings by their countrymen through military conquest. The throne would oftentimes stay within the family. Thus, when you look at the books of Kings, sons were often the successors to the throne. This was the case with Solomon, who was the successor to his father David, and also the case with Christ, who was anointed to sit on the throne of David. Kingdoms and kings are an inseparable part of the fabric of biblical history. There are two Older Testament books dedicated to tracing the life and events of the kings and the kingdoms of Israel, 1 and 2 Kings. The books of 1 and 2 Samuel record and provide some information about the appointment and behavior of the first kings of Israel. First and second Chronicles also record the activities of the kings of Israel. Some of the prophets record activities and events surrounding the kings of Israel. The Newer Testament opens up with a brutal king, Herod the Great. As you can see, the Bible is a kingdom book! This is evident as early as Genesis 14, where the king of Salem is portrayed as a type of Christ. Miriam, after witnessing the parting of the Red Sea, proclaimed, "The LORD shall reign forever and ever" (Exodus 15:18). God is recorded as declaring that He would make Israel a kingdom of priests (Exodus 19:6). The Bible records through the majestic Psalms that God is King, and Isaiah, the prophet, receives a vision of God sitting on the throne (Isaiah 6:1). The backdrop of the scripture is Kingdom, not democratic.

With a long history of subservience under foreign powers (Assyrian, Babylonian, Persian, Greek, and Roman), the Jews came to understand submission to authority as the *sine qua non* for good and peaceful relationship with their political masters. Conquest was all about domination, the conquering nation plundering resources; spreading its religion, culture, and philosophy; and dominating and dictating the terms of the religious, political, and cultural life of the conquered nation. Each kingdom had its own king, its own form of government, military, culture, economic system, laws, and religious practices. This is the kingdom context of the Bible.

The Roman Empire, through taxation, allowed the Jewish kingdom to exist under its control as long as it remained subservient to the economic and political laws of Rome. Jews had to pay their taxes to Caesar, whose image was on the currency of that day. This was the context in which Jesus taught the disciples to render to Caesar the things that are Caesar's and to God the things that are God's, contrasting the two kingdoms (Matthew 22:21). Christ's Kingdom was not of this world, as He told Pilate (John 18:36).

As a learned and well-traveled man, Paul understood the dynamics of the Kingdom of God and its implications for both Jews and Gentiles.

Many of the prophetic monologues and dialogues of the Older Testament, a number of the parables of Jesus, and teachings in the epistles carry a Kingdom message framed in a context dissimilar to our own. Where we are prone to view Kingdom through Western lenses that leave us with the notion of personal rights and individual claims, such a concept is alien to the world of the Newer Testament.

The Early Church Citizens of the Kingdom

When we take a cultural look at scripture, in light of its Kingdom context, the writings of Paul help us to see the embodiment of the message of Christ and His Kingdom. You must remember Christ preached, taught, and demonstrated the Kingdom, so that the disciples could go and express it to the world. Thus, when you look at the epistles, you are not going to find narratives that tell a story; instead you are simply going to discover doctrine that is related to the Kingdom. The gospels provide narratives or stories that depict the life, ministry, and message of Christ and His disciples. The book of Acts also provides narratives that depict the ministry of His disciples who became apostles and others whom the Lord was calling. So, to try to see the clarity of the Kingdom within the doctrine of the epistles, without understanding the context, is almost impossible – the Roman Catholic Church is proof positive of that. So let's take a Kingdom context look at Paul's writing to see if we can discover what perspective Paul, who authored two-thirds of the Newer Testament, wrote from.

Before his conversion, Saul was born both a Jew and a Roman citizen (Acts 16:37-38; 22:25-29; 23:27, Philippians 3:5-6). Paul states in scripture that he was a Roman citizen. Born in Tarsus, which was the capital of the Roman province of Cilicia, Paul probably gained Roman citizenship through service his father rendered to Rome. When Paul was dealing with a citizenship issue of scourging and flogging, which was unlawful to perform on a Roman citizen, he stated that he was a Jew who was a Roman citizen.

> *But when Paul perceived that one part were Sadducees and the other Pharisees, he cried out in the council, "Men and brethren, I am a Pharisee, the son of a Pharisee; concerning the hope and resurrection of the dead I am being judged!" And when he had said this, a dissension arose between the Pharisees and the Sadducees; and the assembly was divided. For Sadducees say that there is no resurrection—and no angel or spirit; but the Pharisees confess both. Then there arose a loud outcry. And the scribes of the Pharisees' party arose and protested, saying, "We find no evil in this man; but if a spirit or an angel has spoken to him, let us not fight against God." – Acts 23:6-9*

Paul understood the weightiness of citizenship, as seen in his ability to finagle his way out of a flogging:

> *And as they bound him with thongs, Paul said to the centurion who stood by, "Is it lawful for you to scourge a man who is a Roman, and uncondemned?" When the centurion heard that, he went and told the commander, saying, "Take care what you do, for this man is a Roman." Then the commander came and said to him, "Tell me, are you a Roman?" He said, "Yes." The commander answered, "With a large sum I obtained this citizenship." And Paul said, "But I was born a citizen." Then immediately those who were about to examine him withdrew from him; and the commander was also afraid after he found out that he was a Roman, and because he had bound him. – Acts 22:25-29*

Citizenship meant everything in the biblical context, and the very fact that Paul argued this issue demonstrated how aware he was of citizenship issues. The Roman centurion, in charge of the incarceration of Paul, said to Paul that he paid a great deal of money to purchase Roman citizenship. This demonstrates how important it was to be under a certain kingdom as a citizen. However, Paul let him know that the centurion paid to become what Paul was born as – a Roman citizen. Therefore, the commander set Paul free. Why? Because citizenship has its privileges! To claim falsely to be a citizen of Rome was a capital offense punishable by death. Citizenship is serious!

A citizen of two kingdoms, Paul enjoyed the best of both worlds. Born in a Jewish family, the offspring of the tribe of Benjamin and circumcised on the eighth day, he considered himself a Hebrew of Hebrews (Philippians 3:5). But this Pharisee who became a student of the famed Jewish scholar Rabban Gamaliel and a member of the Sanhedrin, was also a Roman citizen. Paul would have had three names: *praenomen, nomen,* and *cognomen.* The *cognomen* was like a surname, and in the apostle's case, this was the Latin name *Paullus* (Greek *Paulos*), which identified him as a member of the Paulli family. Luke began to use his Latin name (Acts 13:9), instead of the Hebrew Saul (Shaul, Acts 7:58; 8:1), after the conversion of the Cypriote governor at Paphos during the first missionary journey. This name was more than likely what is called a *supernomen* or nickname. It was common among Jews to take a *supernomen.*

Tarsus, the place of Paul's nativity, was no average city. Its inhabitants were known for their philosophical and education acumen. The students of Tarsus were seen as what we today would call Rhodes scholars; they would study abroad quite frequently. This is how Saul studied with the head Pharisee and scholar, Gamaliel. When you examine the life and ministry of Paul to get an understanding of the message he preached, you must look at his religious background and affiliation.

Paul was a Pharisee of Pharisees, according to his own acknowledgment (Philippians 3:5). Who were the Pharisees? They were a religious group who emerged post-Maccabean revolt, making their first public appearance under the Hasmonean rule in 135-134 BC. The word "Pharisee" is associated with a Hebrew and Aramaic root meaning "separate"; thus, the name means "separate ones." The Pharisees were the largest of the three religious schools of thought among the Jews; the Sadducees and the Essenes being the other two. Unlike the Sadducees, they believed in the resurrection of the dead, angels, and spirits (Acts 23:8). The Sadducees regarded themselves as guardians of the traditional faith of Israel and saw the Pharisees in danger of violating the law by trying to be to contemporary. Thus, the Sadducees saw the Pharisees as dangerous innovators or modernists. The Pharisees were viewed as extremely legalistic and meticulous concerning their pursuits concerning the Law of Moses. There were two leading schools of thought within the group: the school of Shammai (the conservative wing) and the school of Hillel (the liberal wing). As a student of Gamaliel, who was a grandson of Hillel and a member of the liberal wing, in many ways, Paul appeared to be of the Hillelite camp, though his intolerance for Christianity and non-negotiable commitment to Jewish theological orthodoxy is hard to reconcile with this position.

Paul's Pharisaic belief in the resurrection of the dead and the hope of the Messiah made him an ideal candidate to promote the resurrection and Messiahship of Christ. For Paul, this became the first point of faith or belief for the believer. Josephus, the Jewish historian, who was also believed to be a Pharisee and who wrote in ways to appeal to the Greek philosophers and Platonic thought, notes that the Pharisees taught that the soul had power to survive death and that there are rewards and punishments under the earth for those who have led lives of virtue or vice.[1] They believed that there would be eternal imprisonment for lost souls, while the good souls receive an easy passage to a new life. Thus, you can see why Paul would have such a strong emphasis on the resurrection, but it is also clear that he understood the resurrection as the doorway to the Kingdom and the means to new life.

Let's now attempt to look at Paul's understanding of what it means to have a relationship with God through Christ, the scope of his gospel. When we look at these three Pauline epistles – Colossians 1:13-18, Ephesians 2:11-21, and Philippians 3:20 – they give us insight into the cultural context to which we are oblivious. It is understood that Christ was declared King upon His resurrection. We discussed His coronation and riding into Jerusalem on a mule earlier in this book, but it is clear that Christ is the King and the church has been given the keys to the Kingdom.

Salvation is the gateway to the Kingdom and when people are ushered into the Kingdom, they become citizens of the Kingdom, are added to the church, and are entitled to all the rights and privileges of the Kingdom, while being subject to all its laws and obligations. Thus, Paul's emphasis

---

1 Bruce. F.F. (1977). *Paul Apostle of the Heart Set Free,* Carlisle Cumbria: Wm B. Eerdmans Publishing Co., p. 301.

on the resurrection is directly connected to the gospel of the Kingdom; it cannot be disassociated with Christ's message of the Kingdom. The passion and resurrection of Christ is simply the means to citizenship in the Kingdom. Even more so, as Kingdom citizens who constitute His Body, believers enter into Christ's present reign (Ephesians 2:6).

Let's study the scriptures with more detail:

> *He has delivered us from the power of darkness and conveyed us into the kingdom of the Son of His love, in whom we have redemption through His blood, the forgiveness of sins. – Colossians 1:13-14*
>
> *Now, therefore, you are no longer strangers and foreigners, but fellow citizens with the saints and members of the household of God, having been built on the foundation of the apostles and prophets, Jesus Christ Himself being the chief cornerstone, in whom the whole building, being fitted together, grows into a holy temple in the Lord, in whom you also are being built together for a dwelling place of God in the Spirit. – Ephesians 2:19-22*
>
> *Brethren, join in following my example, and note those who so walk, as you have us for a pattern. For many walk, of whom I have told you often, and now tell you even weeping, that they are the enemies of the cross of Christ: whose end is destruction, whose god is their belly, and whose glory is in their shame—who set their mind on earthly things.*
>
> *For our citizenship is in heaven, from which we also eagerly wait for the Savior, the Lord Jesus Christ, who will transform our lowly body that it may be conformed to His glorious body, according to the working by which He is able even to subdue all things to Himself. – Philippians 3:17-21*

It is clear that Paul is writing from the unmentioned context of the Kingdom of God. In Colossians, he states that the believer is one who has been released from the dominion of darkness and Satan and has been transferred to the Kingdom of the Son of His love. This is none other than the Kingdom of God. The early church understood that the good news was that God had inaugurated His Kingdom, and those who come to Him by means of the death, burial, and resurrection of His Son could receive redemption through His blood, forgiveness of sins, and become citizens of His Kingdom. You may be saying, "This is what I have always believed," but the difference is that most people focus upon redemption through the blood and forgiveness of sins and forget about or totally ignore the part about conveying us to the Kingdom of the Son of His love.

Focusing on redemption overlooks the fact that Paul emphasizes deliverance from the power of darkness and conveyance in the Kingdom. However, everything in the passage flows into one complete thought and perfectly goes together. Paul writes that through Christ, we have been delivered, speaking of His work on the cross and His power over death and the grave. He was not referring to His message of the good news of the Kingdom. Hence, Jesus' work on the cross makes the good news of the Kingdom applicable and relevant, for without His vicarious death on the cross, we cannot have access to the Kingdom. Therefore, we have been delivered from the power of Satan if we have received Christ, not only as Savior, but as King.

When Paul writes that Jesus delivered us "from," he is suggesting that you and I were once under the dominion of Satan and darkness. He said Satan dominated us or ruled over us as king. So Paul writes using redemptive language that contextually communicates the Kingdom of God. The word "power" Paul uses here is literally "authority" or *exousia* (ἐξουσία) in the Greek language, which means "the right to rule, or authority, to be unhindered." So, in Pauline understanding, salvation is not simply forgiveness of sin; it is also the conveying or dragging one out of the kingdom of darkness into the Kingdom of God. In the mind of Paul, there is no need of a resurrection without the Kingdom of God. The resurrection is connected to the new birth of the believer, thereby providing the means to the Kingdom of God. Paul's understanding of Kingdom citizenship is even clearer in the Ephesians 2:19-22 passage.

Paul's writings suggest that the redemptive acts of Christ served as a means to citizenship, not simply the forgiveness of sins. A lot of people sadly mistake salvation as God being a good guy who gives the sinner a break by forgiving his or her sin and not holding it against them. We further interpret salvation as mere acknowledgment that Jesus died for our sins and our reservations to heaven are automatically made – there is a seat, room, mansion or whatever we believe waiting for us. We don't have any obligations in this Kingdom – just privileges and complaints when the King doesn't rule in our favor or to our liking. Then, if we really get disappointed with His ways, we can always threaten giving Him up all together. So if He knows what's best for Him and wants to keep us as one of His people, He had better do something about our circumstance or we're out!

Unfortunately, when you only preach the advent and the event of the resurrection, this is the kind of reality that is produced. But Jesus is not simply Savior, He is also Lord – the King of the Kingdom of God. And as the King, He controls who He saves. If He is consumed with your death, you must be consumed with His life. It's an exchange of a life for a life – a death for a death! Paul declared that believers have become citizens of God's Kingdom! Like the Roman centurion of Acts 22:28 declared about his Roman citizenship, our citizenship costs a great deal! Citizenship is important and expensive; Christ paid a large sum in order to naturalize the believer into the Kingdom of God through the power of the resurrection, which gave us new life in Christ (2 Corinthians 5:17).

Paul declared, just as he did in his epistle to the Philippians and Colossians, that he is writing to them as citizens of the Kingdom. Paul then explains the details of how citizenship took place through the cross of Christ and how to govern themselves as citizens. Paul was not writing to a cultural context like ours – be it North America, Africa, Asia, South America, Europe, or Australia. He declares that we are not foreigners or strangers, but fellow citizens of the Kingdom! Remember citizenship was where a person in antiquity received their identity, like Simon the Cyrene, the Roman centurion Cornelius, Jesus the Jew. A person's citizenship gave rise to their identity, rights, privileges. A person's citizenship defined what rule and laws to which they were subject.

There are two words that we must make sure that we do not just skip over, because they express the Kingdom theology of Paul that is missed by modern day Christians – "fellow citizens." While in Greek, we do not refer to this as a compound word, for your sake I will refer to it as a compound word (two words that make up one word). The Greek word is *sumpolites* (συμπολίτης). The first word is *sum* (sun), which implies "closeness or together, with, or together with." The second word, *polites* is from *polis*, which means "city." Thus, *sumpolites* means "a citizen, an inhabitant of a city, one who has the right of citizenship, a freeman." In other words, a fellow citizen, figuratively, refers to Gentile Christians who have become citizens of God's Kingdom family (Ephesians 2:19).[2]

The next word to consider is "saints." This word is the Greek term, *hágios* (ἅγιος), "any matter of religious awe, expiation, sacrifice." It also means "holy, set apart, sanctified, consecrated, saint." It has a common root, *hág-*, with hagnos, which means "chaste or pure." Its fundamental meaning is:

- Separation – Consecration, devotion to the service of deity, sharing in God's purity and abstaining from earth's defilement.
- Pure – Clean, ceremonially or morally clean, including the idea of deserved respect, reverence.

It particularly means perfect, without blemish (Romans 12:1). Metaphorically, it means morally pure, upright, blameless in heart and life, virtuous, holy (Mark 6:20, Romans 7:12, 1 Corinthians 7:34, Ephesians 1:4; 5:27, 1 Peter 1:16, Septuagint: Leviticus 11:44); it is spoken of those who are purified and sanctified by the influences of the Spirit. This is assumed of all who profess the Christian name, hence *hágios*, saint, *hágioi*, saints, or Christians (Acts 9:13-14, 32, 41; 26:10, Romans 1:7; 8:27, 1 Thessalonians 3:13) or those who are to be in any way included in the Christian community (1 Corinthians 7:14). Holy kiss means the sacred Christian kiss, the pledge of Christian affection (Romans 16:16, 1 Corinthians 16:20, 2 Corinthians 13:12). Another definition for "saints" or *hágioi* is consecrated: devoted, sacred, holy, meaning set apart from a common to a sacred use; spoken of places, temples, cities, the priesthood, men (Matthew 4:5; 7:6; 24:15; 27:53, Acts 6:13; 7:33); of firstfruits (Romans 11:16); of a male open-

2 Zodhiates, S. (2000). The Complete Word Study Dictionary: New Testament (electronic ed.). Chattanooga, TN: AMG Publishers.

ing the womb (Luke 2:23); of apostles (Ephesians 3:5); of prophets (Luke 1:70, Acts 3:21, 2 Peter 1:21); of angels (Matthew 25:31).[3]

The proper definition of saints is the name for believers meaning "holy ones" (which is the rendering in some modern versions). The Older Testament believers were called to be "holy," or consecrated to God (Exodus 22:31, Leviticus 11:44). In the Newer Testament, "saints" became the Apostle Paul's favorite name for Christians (Romans 1:7; 8:27; 12:13; 15:25-26, 31; 16:2, 15; plus 31 other places in Paul's letters).[4] The name indicates that Christians are expected to be holy (Hebrews 12:10, Revelation 22:11), because they have been consecrated to God as a holy priesthood and have rejected the ways of the world (1 Peter 1:15-16; 2:5, 9). More than that, they are the people of the coming age, who will reign with God over the earth and over angels.[5] Thus, to the Philippians, Paul writes:

> *Brethren, join in following my example, and note those who so walk, as you have us for a pattern. For many walk, of whom I have told you often, and now tell you even weeping, that they are the enemies of the cross of Christ: whose end is destruction, whose god is their belly, and whose glory is in their shame—who set their mind on earthly things. For our citizenship is in heaven, from which we also eagerly wait for the Savior, the Lord Jesus Christ, who will transform our lowly body that it may be conformed to His glorious body, according to the working by which He is able even to subdue all things to Himself. – Philippians 3:17-21*

In this passage, Paul discusses the expectation of appropriate Kingdom behavior. He understands that many may not understand Kingdom principles and practices of behavior and offers his life as an example. He calls his life a pattern – a pattern of what? Judaism? Of course not, but a pattern of behavior of this new Kingdom that Christ made available through His death on the cross. It is clear that he is referring to the Kingdom of God and the expected behavior that should be the culture of the Kingdom that he himself was modeling. He contrasted his behavior with those who say

---

3 Ibid.

4 Elwell, W. A., & Comfort, P. W. (2001), *Tyndale Bible Dictionary*, Tyndale reference library (1150–1151), Wheaton, Ill.: Tyndale House Publishers.

5 Ibid.

that they have a relationship with Christ and are a part of His Kingdom, but their belly is their god. He also said their glory is in their shame and they set their minds on earthly things or the kingdoms of this world, rather than the Kingdom of God. Paul is so clear in this passage that he refers to those who are living according to the patterns of this world as enemies to the cross. Wow! An enemy to the cross, just because you want to live according to your own ideas, ideals, dreams, and desires? The cross of Christ was supposed to be the place of death, the place that sinners plunge beneath the blood and are washed from their guilt and shame, and then the Spirit of God gives them a new life with new passions, not sins forgiven with the same passions.

In the abridged collection and summary of His teaching on the Kingdom – what Matthew calls the "Sermon on the Mount" (chapters 5-7) and Luke calls the "Sermon on the Plain" (chapter 6) – Jesus describes the character and conduct of His followers, Kingdom citizens, whether an individual or community, under Christ's rule and Lordship. A recurring note throughout the sermon is the counter-culture life, the life of contrast that Kingdom citizens must live in the midst of a decadent society. Jesus makes clear that Kingdom citizens must speak the language and live lives consistent with the palace.

The sermon, both in Matthew and Luke, summons believers to a life of radical discipleship: "For I tell you that unless your righteousness surpasses that of the Pharisees and the teachers of the law, you will certainly not enter the kingdom of heaven" (Matthew 5:20). "Why do you call me, 'Lord, Lord,' and do not do what I say?" (Luke 6:46). There is such a serious misunderstanding of grace among the people of God today. God's people need to understand that grace does not permit what the law condemns. It offers forgiveness where the law only condemns, but does not condone sin. In a sense, grace demands more than the law, because it provides the power to do what God commands.

Let us get back to Paul in Philippians 3:17-19. The cross of Christ is the place of crossing out and cross-over; through the cross, the sinful past can be blotted out for every person who believes in Jesus. But the cross also provides an opportunity to crossover from the dominion of Satan and the passions of the flesh to the dominion of God with the appetites of the Spirit. Paul urges that a person's desires ought to change as a result of the cross. He firmly states that our citizenship is in heaven, from which we also eagerly wait for the Savior, the Lord Jesus Christ.

Note Paul is now moving into the discussion of both the hope of the return of Christ and the resurrection of the dead, which is associated with his theology of the Kingdom. He refers to Christ the Savior, but then immediately refers to Him as the Lord Jesus Christ. Paul makes a clear distinction between Savior and Lord that we miss today. Too many simply understand Christ as Savior, which allows them to dichotomize the event of the cross and resurrection from the gospel of the Kingdom. Jesus is Savior because He died, but He is Lord because He is risen from the dead. His resurrection empowers Him to vindicate His claims and promises made to us. His resurrection and ascension to heaven authorize Him to reign as King and Lord of all. Unfortunately, many modern Christians simply see Him as Savior, but not Lord and have become enemies of the cross, because they have not died to themselves or their fleshly passions and have not submitted their lives to His Lordship (Romans 10:9-10, Colossians 3:1).

In the mind of Paul, Christ must be Lord and Savior. Let's examine a very familiar passage of scripture he wrote to the church in Rome:

> *But what does it say. "The word is near you, in your mouth and in your heart" (that is, the word of faith which we preach): that if you confess with your mouth the Lord Jesus and believe in your heart that God has raised Him from the dead, you will be saved. For with the heart one believes unto righteousness, and with the mouth confession is made unto salvation. For the Scripture says, "Whoever believes on Him will not be put to shame." For there is no distinction between Jew and Greek, for the same Lord over all is rich to all who call upon Him. For "whoever calls on the name of the Lord shall be saved." – Romans 10:8-13*

If you have been in or around the church or church people, surely you have heard this passage before, but if not, I'm going to explain it to you. Let's take a look at the first part of this pericope:

> *But what does it say. "The word is near you, in your mouth and in your heart" (that is, the word of faith which we preach): that if you confess with your mouth the Lord Jesus and believe in your heart that God has raised Him from the dead, you will be saved.*

Paul explained to the believers in Rome that the Lord Jesus is the way to salvation and a relationship with God the King. Paul explained in chapter 10 how Christ is the end of the law for righteousness to everyone who believes in His message and ministry of the Kingdom by way of the cross. He addressed judgment through the ministry of Christ and culminated with how to access God through Christ. Thus, he stated that you must confess with your mouth the Lord Jesus. To confess the Lord Jesus is to acknowledge Him as your King or Lord. Let's look at the Greek word "confess." The Greek term for "confess" is *homologéo* (ὁμολογέω), contracted *homologó*, which is from *homo*, which means "together with" and *logos*, which means "to say." Thus, *homologéo* means "to assent, consent, admit, as used commonly in classical Greek; to promise, i.e., to agree with or consent to the desire of another."[6] So Paul states that the way to the Kingdom and salvation is to first confess Christ as your new King and Master. Paul says that we must give over to Him in confession, which is "to say the same thing about Christ that He says about Himself and say the same thing about yourself that He says about you." He is Lord and King of the Kingdom of God. You and I are sinners who were worthy of death, but the goodness of the King came and liberated us from the power of sin and bondage; He liberated us from the power of Satan to the power of God (Acts 26:18, Colossians 1:13). Therefore, Paul says that we must confess the Lord Jesus; he states clearly that Jesus is Lord without question.

Let's look at the Greek word for "Lord." The Greek term for "Lord" is *kurios* (κύριος), which means "might, power, Lord, master, owner." *Kurios* is also the Newer Testament Greek equivalent for the Older Testament Hebrew term Jehovah.[7] To confess Christ as Lord is to declare Him as your supreme ruler and authority, master and owner. This is Kingdom of God language. The people of that day understood that to acknowledge Christ as

6 Zodhiates, S. (2000). *The Complete Word Study Dictionary: New Testament* (electronic ed.). Chattanooga, TN: AMG Publishers.
7 Ibid.

Lord was to declare Him as their King. This was an important issue during this era in which the king owned all the land and resources of his kingdom and required people to pay a tribute of taxes to him for their use. His was the prerogative to seize land and property without recourse.

Since Caesar was considered to be lord, master, potentate, or king, to confess Christ as King was like committing high treason, if you were living within the provinces of the Roman Empire. So when Paul said that they should confess Christ as Lord, he was requesting them to make Christ king over Caesar the emperor. This monumental statement makes the writing in Romans 12 and 13 make sense. In Romans 12, Paul demands that in light of what Christ has done for us by granting us access to the Kingdom of God through His death and resurrection, it only makes sense to present our bodies a living sacrifice unto Him. This is our intelligent service and dedication to our King. However, he then writes in chapter 13 to let every soul be subject to the governing authorities. For there is no authority except from God, and the authorities who exist do so by the permission of God. Paul was giving crucial parameters on how to live as both Kingdom citizens and Roman citizens. He admonished the Romans Christians (and us) to obey the powers that be, as long as they do not infringe upon the Lordship of Christ.

So this passage begins by admonishing us to confess Christ the Lord, then believe that God has raised Him from the dead. Paul here addresses two subject matters very dear to his heart as a former Pharisee: the hope of the Messiah and the resurrection of the dead. Paul says that we should confess that Christ the King gained dominion over sin, death, and the grave through His finished work on the cross, and God raised Him from the dead!

I think that this is an excellent time to discuss Pauline anthropology and soteriology. This is germane to the effects of Christ's death on the cross and the good news of the Kingdom. The fact that Paul states that God raised Jesus from the dead, which is a consistent theme in the writings of Paul, gives us insight to Paul's perspective on the humanity of Christ. The fact that Paul says that God raised Jesus from the dead suggests that Paul was acknowledging the humanity of Christ. Paul understood the necessity of Christ being fully God and fully man; thus, in Romans 5 and 1 Corinthians 15, he refers to Christ as the last Adam. In Paul's epistle to the Philippians in chapter 2, which is referred to as the kenosis chapter, Paul discusses how Christ veiled His divinity and took on the form of a man. In Galatians, Paul writes that God sent forth His Son born of a woman, which highlights His humanity (Galatians 4:4). Pauline anthropology is based upon Adam being the federal and seminal head of humanity, and when the first Adam disobeyed God, all of humanity fell within his loins and genes. All of humanity came through the bloodline of Adam. All of humanity is born through the bloodline of Adam and suffers from the proclivities of his fallen nature. Therefore, all of humanity in the entire world is in need of a Savior. Jesus is referred to as the last Adam, who in turn did not sin, but encountered the same devil and resisted him. Though He was tempted, He demonstrated spiritual restraint and defeated Satan. Jesus was not born through the genes of Adam because He was born of a virgin, not through the seed of Joseph. This allowed Jesus not to be marred by the same sinful propensities and sin nature as the rest of humanity. His divine sonship and unfallen nature qualified Him to be the gate to a new creation in which, having been forgiven of our sins, we may walk by faith in God who loves us.

When Paul states that Jesus was raised from the dead, this too was laced with Jewish thought and culture. Israel's worship to God the King revolved around the Jewish feasts. The resurrection and the effects thereof cannot fully be understood and appreciated without some understanding of the first journey of Israel. Israel was commanded by God to travel three times a year to a holy convocation with the Lord (Deuteronomy 16:16). There were seven feasts, and they were celebrated in three journeys. The first journey celebrated three feasts: Passover, Unleavened Bread, and Firstfruits. The second journey was a stand-alone feast – Pentecost or Feast of Weeks and the last journey celebrated the Atonement or Yom Kippur, Trumpets, and Tabernacles. The first journey was the foundation for the sacrifice of Christ: Passover and Firstfruits were the foundation for the resurrection. These Jewish feasts were instituted by God and were a type and a shadow of that which was to come. These feasts focused upon the perspective of God as King, who would meet them once a year at the mercy seat, which was the earthly throne of God. Paul was a Jew and understood the fulfillment of the feasts in Christ Jesus. Thus, Jesus is the King, the perfect sacrifice who saves!

Paul's soteriology or understanding of salvation is intimately connected to His anthropology. Thus, he declares:

> *...that if you confess with your mouth the Lord Jesus and believe in your heart that God has raised Him from the dead, you will be saved. – Romans 10:9*

Paul wrote that those who confess Christ as their personal Lord and King and believe that God has raised Him from the dead will be saved from eternal punishment. He asserted that this is only possible by faith in both the Kingship and saving work of Christ. Righteousness is a declaration of the King that is issued through a believing heart and a confessing mouth. Kingdom citizens must continue to have faith in the declaration of the King and publicly express their allegiance to His Lordship.

There is no distinction between the good news of the Kingdom that Jesus preached and the gospel that the apostle's preached; it is the same message. Christ inaugurated the Kingdom through preaching, teaching, and demonstrating of the gospel of the Kingdom, and the apostles spread that message in a context that understood the connection between the resurrection and the Kingdom of God. They understood that the resurrection of Christ, as the Firstfruits, became the firstfruits of them that slept (1 Corinthians 15:20), which is stated in the Pauline epistles. Christ's resurrection from the dead was the passageway to the Kingdom of God. Christ proclaimed the Kingdom, explained the Kingdom, and demonstrated the Kingdom. But through His death and resurrection, He made available the Kingdom – an open invitation to perpetual fellowship with God through His own blood! Thank God for the ministry of Christ, for we are now members of the household of God and fellow citizens with the saints.

7

Paul's Gospel

In this chapter, I want do a closer examination of Paul's understanding of the gospel and address the question, "Was Paul's gospel different than the gospel that Jesus preached?" Undoubtedly, Paul was a Kingdom preacher. Christ arrested him on the road to Damascus and revealed Himself to Paul as the Messiah (Acts 9:1-9). The conversion and encounter of Paul with Christ was an affirmation that Jesus was the Messiah.

When we consider the Pharisaic background of Paul, which included a strong Messianic hope, the resurrection of the dead, and an expectation of the Kingdom of God, the ministry and message of Christ was not foreign to Paul. Although he initially did not believe that He was the Messiah and the fulfillment of the Older Testament prophecies, Paul believed in the things that Christ presented. When Christ introduced Himself to him on the Damascus road as Jesus, whom he was persecuting, everything fell into place in Paul's mind and he yielded himself to God:

> *Then Saul, still breathing threats and murder against the disciples of the Lord, went to the high priest and asked letters from him to the synagogues of Damascus, so that if he found any who were of the Way, whether men or women, he might bring them bound to Jerusalem. As he journeyed he came near Damascus, and suddenly a light shone around him from heaven. Then he fell to the ground, and heard a voice saying to him, "Saul, Saul, why are you persecuting Me?" And he said, "Who are You, Lord?" Then the*

Lord said, "I am Jesus, whom you are persecuting. It is hard for you to kick against the goads." So he, trembling and astonished, said, "Lord, what do You want me to do?" Then the Lord said to him, "Arise and go into the city, and you will be told what you must do." – Acts 9:1-6

Some scholars argue that Saul's conversion experience began with the stoning of Stephen, whose courage, cogent argument, and willingness to die for his conviction that Jesus was Messiah, inspired and goaded him. Paul was one of the most zealous Pharisees during that time. His conversion on the road to Damascus began the most significant moves in the early church. After his encounter with Jesus on the road, Paul was instructed to go to Ananias, who laid hands on him and restored his sight. From him, he received clarity for his future ministry. Paul did not have to be doctrinally convinced concerning the message of Christ; he just needed to be assured that the advent of the Messiah had taken place. That would release a fierce faith in Christ. Luke records:

Then Ananias answered, "Lord, I have heard from many about this man, how much harm he has done to Your saints in Jerusalem. And here he has authority from the chief priests to bind all who call on Your name." But the Lord said to him, "Go, for he is a chosen vessel of Mine to bear My name before Gentiles, kings, and the children of Israel. For I will show him how many things he must suffer for My name's sake." And Ananias went his way and entered the house; and laying his hands on him he said, "Brother Saul, the Lord Jesus, who appeared to you on the road as you came, has sent me that you may receive your sight and be filled with the Holy Spirit." Immediately there fell from his eyes something like scales, and he received his sight at once; and he arose and was baptized. So when he had received food, he was strengthened. Then Saul spent some days with the disciples at Damascus. Immediately he preached the Christ in the synagogues, that He is the Son of God. Then all who heard were amazed, and said, "Is this not he who destroyed those who called on this name in Jerusalem, and has come here for that purpose, so that he might bring them bound to the chief priests?" But Saul increased all the more in strength, and confounded the Jews who dwelt in Damascus, proving that this Jesus is the Christ. – Acts 9:13-22

Due to Paul's thorough training in Judaism, he was well aware of the Older Testament prophecies, and since Christ fulfilled them, 100% of them, it was easy for Paul to preach Jesus the Messiah once his spiritual eyes were opened!

> *"Do not think that I came to destroy the Law or the Prophets. I did not come to destroy but to fulfill. – Matthew 5:17*

After Paul spent some time with the disciples, and were taught the teachings of Jesus, the Messianic secrets, and things concerning His advent and resurrection, Paul became a powerful firearm for the Kingdom of God. Paul's gospel *was* the gospel of the Kingdom, for that is what Jesus commanded His disciples to preach. But his message was about the Kingdom, because the Older Testament prophecies promised and the Jews expected that the coming deliverer would be Messiah ben David, Messiah son of David, the most illustrious king of Israel. As with Jesus, Paul's portrayal of the Kingdom, however, was God's spiritual reign.

You do not hear Paul use the word "kingdom" as much, because it was understood that if the Messiah had come in the person of Jesus, so had the Kingdom. Historically and prophetically, it was known that the Messiah had come to inaugurate the Kingdom age, of which Paul and his hearers were very aware. So when Paul did speak of the gospel, it was understood that it was the gospel of the Kingdom. And when he spoke of the advent and the resurrection, it was the good news of the validation of Jesus' Messiahship and the establishment of the Kingdom age.

The question of whether or not Paul's gospel was only the death, burial, and resurrection of Christ as opposed to Christ's gospel of the dominion of God is unnecessary. Christ on the Damascus road appointed Saul to carry His message, perpetuate His ministry, and bring His mission to the Gentile world! Now, Paul was appointed to not only preach the gospel of Kingdom of God futuristically, but to affirm its inauguration through Christ the Messiah. The Jewish people did not disagree with the concept of the Messiah, the Kingdom, or the resurrection of the dead; they just did not believe that Christ was that Messiah.

Christ the Messiah was at the center of Paul's ministry. God was strategic in preserving Saul, one of the most passionate men for Judaism and the law – a Pharisee, thus an avid believer in the resurrection who hoped for the Messiah, to confirm Jesus' Messiahship. Paul's encounter with Christ was significant, because he personally had to be convinced, without a shadow of a doubt, that Jesus was the Messiah. Remember – in the Kingdom context of both the Jews and Gentiles, the preaching and teachings of Jesus were highly offensive; thus, Saul (a Jew and a Roman) religiously and ruthlessly persecuted the church, labeling it as an apostate, heretical sect led by an evil man, who had the nerve to think He was a king.

Paul, after encountering Jesus, had a two-fold mission: 1) to confirm Jesus as the Messiah and 2) to preach the Kingdom. The content of the Kingdom message came by revelation of the Hebrew scriptures and the teachings of Christ, that were handed down to Paul. The Messiahship of Jesus was confirmed through His mission as the Passover Lamb and Firstfruits of the dead. When you read the epistles of Paul, you encounter the word "gospel." However, you must understand the cultural and theological context in which he wrote. Presenting Christ as the Passover Lamb was Paul's authentication of His Messiahship. Paul was forced to defend and argue Christ's Messiahship from this prophetic basis in several vicious encounters with other Jews. The Messiah ushered in the Kingdom; you cannot have the Kingdom without the Messiah, and vice versa. Jesus, as the Messiah, was confirmed King in the resurrection.

The next thing Paul was called to address was Christ's teachings on the Kingdom of God. Paul was called to shift the Jews' understanding of the Kingdom from a Jewish kingdom to a universal Kingdom for all mankind. The Kingdom of God was not just a political kingdom for the Jews, but a spiritual and everlasting Kingdom of God that will dominate completely in the end. Judaism was always the vehicle for the restoration of the entire world; thus, the return of the Messiah will be the fulfillment of the last Jewish feast, Tabernacles, which will usher in His Millennial Reign and appearance to the Jewish people as the Messiah, Passover Lamb, Power of Pentecost, and the eternal King.

Let's look at some of the popular passages where Paul discusses the gospel from these perspectives on the affirmation of Messiahship through the resurrection of the dead, the good news of the Kingdom age (rule and reign of God), and eternity in the Kingdom age.

> *Moreover, brethren, I declare to you the gospel which I preached to you, which also you received and in which you stand, by which also you are saved, if you hold fast that word which I preached to you—unless you believed in vain. For I delivered to you first of all that which I also received: that Christ died for our sins according to the Scriptures, and that He was buried, and that He rose again the third day according to the Scriptures, and that He was seen by Cephas, then by the twelve. After that He was seen by over five hundred brethren at once, of whom the greater part remain to the present, but some have fallen asleep. After that He was seen by James, then by all the apostles. Then last of all He was seen by me also, as by one born out of due time. For I am the least of the apostles, who am not worthy to be called an apostle, because I persecuted the church of God. But by the grace of God I am what I am, and His grace toward me was not in vain; but I labored more abundantly than they all, yet not I, but the grace of God which was with me. Therefore, whether it was I or they, so we preach and so you believed. – 1 Corinthians 15:1-11*

Paul's first stage of his conversion was the affirmation of Christ the Messiah. As a Pharisee, he already believed in the hope of the Messiah to come, who would sit upon the throne of David and reign as King of the world. He believed in the resurrection of the dead. So conversion truth #1 was that Jesus was the fulfillment of prophecy, the Messiah, and confirmed by His resurrection. In the text above, Paul argued that there were many witnesses, including himself on the Damascus road. Therefore, Paul begins his argument of the gospel with the affirmation of Messiahship, which would have been in the mind of his readers. Jesus' resurrection was proof of the inauguration of the Kingdom of God, not a replacement, or another gospel. Paul preached that you must believe that Jesus was the Messiah and if you believe this, then you understand that He ushered in His Kingdom age, and you now qualify for Kingdom citizenship through the advent and event of His resurrection from the dead (Christ the Passover Lamb and

Firstfruits). Notice, Paul is not arguing that a person should just believe in the advent. The Passover, which is our redemption and the firstfruits, is our gateway to the Kingdom and simply step one in a three-fold salvation experience: salvation, sanctification, and glorification, which implies Kingdom reign and rule. We are now under the dominion of the King, not simply saved from hell; we are being transformed to be conformed to the image of His Son, the King of the Kingdom, the Messiah.

Now let's continue our train of Kingdom thought and consider the flow of Paul's gospel argument in this chapter:

> *Now if Christ is preached that He has been raised from the dead, how do some among you say that there is no resurrection of the dead? But if there is no resurrection of the dead, then Christ is not risen. And if Christ is not risen, then our preaching is empty and your faith is also empty. Yes, and we are found false witnesses of God, because we have testified of God that He raised up Christ, whom He did not raise up—if in fact the dead do not rise. For if the dead do not rise, then Christ is not risen. And if Christ is not risen, your faith is futile; you are still in your sins! Then also those who have fallen asleep in Christ have perished. If in this life only we have hope in Christ, we are of all men the most pitiable. But now Christ is risen from the dead, and has become the firstfruits of those who have fallen asleep. For since by man came death, by Man also came the resurrection of the dead. For as in Adam all die, even so in Christ all shall be made alive. But each one in his own order: Christ the firstfruits, afterward those who are Christ's at His coming. Then comes the end, when He delivers the Kingdom to God the Father, when He puts an end to all rule and all authority and power. For He must reign till He has put all enemies under His feet. The last enemy that will be destroyed is death. For "He has put all things under His feet." But when He says "all things are put under Him," it is evident that He who put all things under Him is excepted. Now when all things are made subject to Him, then the Son Himself will also be subject to Him who put all things under Him, that God may be all in all. – 1 Corinthians 15:12-28*

Now Paul argues the resurrection, implying that if Christ was not raised from the dead, then He is not the Messiah. The Kingdom age could not have begun, and preaching was empty or lacked substance. Paul declared that the resurrection of the dead was the affirmation of the Messiahship of Christ and the official invitation to Kingdom citizenship. Thus, he refers to the Feast of Firstfruits as the foundation for understanding the resurrection as the gateway to the Kingdom for humanity.

> *But now Christ is risen from the dead, and has become the firstfruits of those who have fallen asleep. For since by man came death, by Man also came the resurrection of the dead. For as in Adam all die, even so in Christ all shall be made alive. But each one in his own order: Christ the firstfruits, afterward those who are Christ's at His coming. – 1 Corinthians 15:20-23*

Paul then accelerates his argument by saying that God, through Christ, was subjugating death unto Himself, and will ultimately do away with all rules, powers, and authority when the new heaven and new earth emerges in the full manifestation of the Kingdom of God. Then comes the end, when He delivers the Kingdom to God the Father, when He puts an end to all rule and all authority and power.

> *Then comes the end, when He delivers the Kingdom to God the Father, when He puts an end to all rule and all authority and power. For He must reign till He has put all enemies under His feet. The last enemy that will be destroyed is death. For "He has put all things under His feet." But when He says "all things are put under Him," it is evident that He who put all things under Him is excepted. Now when all things are made subject to Him, then the Son Himself will also be subject to Him who put all things under Him, that God may be all in all. – 1 Corinthians 15:24-28*

Though Paul is not preaching the gospel of the Kingdom in this text, he was arguing the authenticity of Jesus as the Messiah, affirmed by the resurrection. As a doctrinal man, Paul emphasized the resurrection of the dead, which is the gateway to the Kingdom, and without it, we cannot enter the Kingdom.

Paul also discusses a bit of eschatology in that he is discussing the end of this age and the age to come. He discusses the reign of Christ as King and how He will eventually do away with all of the opposing forces to the Kingdom of God. Paul is discussing the Kingdom through and beyond the resurrection, which is the good news, the reign of God. The focal message is the rule and reign of God as King over all of His creation. He demonstrated His worthiness to reign as King over you by His vicarious death on the cross and being raised from the dead. Thus, Christ has dominion over sin, death, and the grave!

When Christ was raised from the dead, He demonstrated that He had dominion over the strongest enemy of humanity – death. Both physical death and spiritual death were the consequence of the fall of man and the tools that Satan now uses to rule and reign in the lives of men. The cross of Christ and resurrection conquered both spiritual and physical death and removed the eternal distance between humankind and God. Thus, Christ is King of kings and Lord of lords! He is *Yeshua Hamashiach*, the anointed one of God.

Chapter 15 in Paul's letter to the church in Corinth is not about the death, burial, and resurrection of Christ – this chapter proclaims that Jesus is the Messiah, as demonstrated through the fulfillment of Passover, Unleavened Bread, and Firstfruits. Because many are both ignorant and uncomfortable about the reign of God in our lives, they argue that the gospel is only that Jesus died for man's sins and rose on the third day for sin, so I'm saved... and that's it. This is a 'sloppy agape' that suggests that all we have to do is simply acknowledge that Jesus is our substitution for sin and we are in. The death, burial, and resurrection of Christ is only the beginning of a spiritual life in the Kingdom of God, and in and of itself, does not provide any direction for a relationship with Christ.

> *And so it is written, "The first man Adam became a living being." The last Adam became a life-giving spirit. However, the spiritual is not first, but the natural, and afterward the spiritual. The first man was of the earth, made of dust; the second Man is the Lord from heaven. As was the man of dust, so also are those who are made of dust; and as is the heavenly Man, so also are those who*

are heavenly. And as we have borne the image of the man of dust, we shall also bear the image of the heavenly Man. Now this I say, brethren, that flesh and blood cannot inherit the Kingdom of God; nor does corruption inherit incorruption. Behold, I tell you a mystery: We shall not all sleep, but we shall all be changed— in a moment, in the twinkling of an eye, at the last trumpet. For the trumpet will sound, and the dead will be raised incorruptible, and we shall be changed. For this corruptible must put on incorruption, and this mortal must put on immortality. So when this corruptible has put on incorruption, and this mortal has put on immortality, then shall be brought to pass the saying that is written: "Death is swallowed up in victory."

"O Death, where is your sting? O Hades, where is your victory?"

The sting of death is sin, and the strength of sin is the law. But thanks be to God, who gives us the victory through our Lord Jesus Christ. Therefore, my beloved brethren, be steadfast, immovable, always abounding in the work of the Lord, knowing that your labor is not in vain in the Lord. – 1 Corinthians 15:45-58

At the end of the chapter, Paul shares that Jesus was God incarnate, who became the last Adam, a life-giving spirit. He argued that our ultimate destination is in the final realm of the Kingdom; now we simply experience manifestations of the Kingdom and live in the Kingdom from an internal perspective. But there will be the coming of a physical aspect of the Kingdom in the eschaton. He also states that flesh and blood cannot inherit the Kingdom of God, hence the need for glorification or the process of mortality being swallowed up by immortality. At the end of life, death will be swallowed up in victory, the grave will have no victory, and death has no sting!

Paul demonstrated the depth of the power and authority of the Messiah and encourages the Kingdom citizen to be loyal and faithful to their King, knowing that everything we see and experience is not meaningless. Let's look at another passage of scripture, which demonstrates Paul's fervor to teach that Jesus was the Messiah:

> *After these things Paul departed from Athens and went to Corinth. And he found a certain Jew named Aquila, born in Pontus, who had recently come from Italy with his wife Priscilla (because Claudius had commanded all the Jews to depart from Rome); and he came to them. So, because he was of the same trade, he stayed with them and worked; for by occupation they were tentmakers. And he reasoned in the synagogue every Sabbath, and persuaded both Jews and Greeks. When Silas and Timothy had come from Macedonia, Paul was compelled by the Spirit, and testified to the Jews that Jesus is the Christ. But when they opposed him and blasphemed, he shook his garments and said to them, "Your blood be upon your own heads; I am clean. From now on I will go to the Gentiles." And he departed from there and entered the house of a certain man named Justus, one who worshiped God, whose house was next door to the synagogue. Then Crispus, the ruler of the synagogue, believed on the Lord with all his household. And many of the Corinthians, hearing, believed and were baptized. Now the Lord spoke to Paul in the night by a vision, "Do not be afraid, but speak, and do not keep silent; for I am with you, and no one will attack you to hurt you; for I have many people in this city." And he continued there a year and six months, teaching the word of God among them. – Acts 18:1-11*

This text reveals Paul's frustration with his countrymen who believed in the coming of the Messiah and the inauguration of the Kingdom, but refused to believe that Jesus was Him. *The greatest instrument, tool, and weapon that Paul had to argue Jesus was the Messiah was providing proof of His resurrection.* Thus, when Paul explains the resurrection, he was not arguing that this was what Jesus preached; he was arguing that this is who Jesus is – *Yeshua Hamashiach*, Jesus the Messiah. Historically recorded in this letter and in Acts, this was one of the main struggles he suffered with in his ministry in Corinth – Jewish disbelief that Jesus was the Messiah. This is why in the epistle to the Corinthians he so eloquently explained how the resurrection proved Jesus was the Passover Lamb and Firstfruits. He also consistently referred the Jews back to their belief in the resurrection of the dead, which was a strong Pharisaical conviction.

I marvel that you are turning away so soon from Him who called you in the grace of Christ, to a different gospel, which is not another; but there are some who trouble you and want to pervert the gospel of Christ. But even if we, or an angel from heaven, preach any other gospel to you than what we have preached to you, let him be accursed. As we have said before, so now I say again, if anyone preaches any other gospel to you than what you have received, let him be accursed. For do I now persuade men, or God? Or do I seek to please men? For if I still pleased men, I would not be a bondservant of Christ. – Galatians 1:6-10

For Paul, the gospel of the Kingdom was strictly connected to Christ – the fulfillment of the Passover, Unleavened Bread, and Firstfruits. In Galatia, there were Judaizers, also called Jewish Christians, who were perverting the gospel of the Kingdom (compelling the Gentiles to adopt Jewish customs). Paul argues otherwise; that the Kingdom must be inaugurated by the Messiah alone who fulfilled Passover, Unleavened Bread, and Firstfruits. John the baptizing one saw Him from a far and said, "Behold the Lamb of God who takes away the sins of the world." The Jewish Christians were saying that Jesus inaugurated the Kingdom, but could not forgive sin; therefore, one must keep the law. However, Christ was both the end and fulfillment of the law. So Paul let them know that Christ is the gateway to the Kingdom, and without His sinless life, His vicarious death on the cross, and His bodily resurrection, there is no entrance to the Kingdom or affirmation of His Messiahship.

So when they had appointed him a day, many came to him at his lodging, to whom he explained and solemnly testified of the kingdom of God, persuading them concerning Jesus from both the Law of Moses and the Prophets, from morning till evening. And some were persuaded by the things which were spoken, and some disbelieved. So when they did not agree among themselves, they departed after Paul had said one word: "The Holy Spirit spoke rightly through Isaiah the prophet to our fathers, saying, 'Go to this people and say:

"Hearing you will hear, and shall not understand;
And seeing you will see, and not perceive;
For the hearts of this people have grown dull.

Their ears are hard of hearing,
And their eyes they have closed,
Lest they should see with their eyes and hear with their ears,
Lest they should understand with their hearts and turn,
So that I should heal them." '

"Therefore let it be known to you that the salvation of God has been sent to the Gentiles, and they will hear it!" And when he had said these words, the Jews departed and had a great dispute among themselves. Then Paul dwelt two whole years in his own rented house, and received all who came to him, preaching the kingdom of God and teaching the things which concern the Lord Jesus Christ with all confidence, no one forbidding him. – Acts 28:23-31

The book of Acts is the history of the Newer Testament church; it is a description of how the disciples understood and practiced the message of Christ. Thus, it records that the preaching of the Kingdom and the things concerning Christ were the focal point of the apostolic ministry. They taught the Kingdom of God as Christ taught it to them and the things concerning Christ as the Messiah. Luke records that for two years, in his own rented house, Paul focused on and preached the Kingdom of God and the things concerning the Lord Jesus Christ. The Kingdom is the sphere where those who are in relationship with God exist. The Kingdom is the rule and reign of God in the hearts of men, which is the present realm of God. The things concerning Christ are: the fulfillment of the Passover, Unleavened Bread, and Firstfruits, the fulfillment of the type and shadow of the Tabernacle, and the feasts and the fulfillment of the Messianic prophecies. Christ is *Yeshua Hamashiach*! It is very clear that Paul's message or gospel was the gospel of the Kingdom, by way of Jesus the Messiah. The concept of Kingdom or Kingdom citizenship is present in all of Paul's general and pastoral epistles. As difficult as it may seem and sound, we have not heard, in our contemporary context, this gospel of the Kingdom.

In Romans, Paul states:

> *Therefore do not let your good be spoken of as evil; for the Kingdom of God is not eating and drinking, but righteousness and peace and joy in the Holy Spirit. For he who serves Christ in these things is acceptable to God and approved by men. – Romans 14:16-18*

Of course, Paul was talking about not eating in the presence of a brother those things that will cause him to stumble because of his immaturity. But I'm simply focusing on the fact that Paul's statements demonstrate, once again, his Kingdom focus. Paul is once again connecting the works of Christ as the means to entering the Kingdom through Christ the Passover Lamb.

Paul's gospel is the gospel of the Kingdom, which he passionately argued was inaugurated in the ministry of Christ.

Luke's writing once again demonstrates the focus of Paul's gospel as he visits the synagogues in Ephesus, as well as the school of Tyrannus for two years. He taught in the synagogue and the academy the things concerning the Kingdom of God and the Lord Jesus or Jesus the Messiah and King.

> *And he went into the synagogue and spoke boldly for three months, reasoning and persuading concerning the things of the kingdom of God. But when some were hardened and did not believe, but spoke evil of the Way before the multitude, he departed from them and withdrew the disciples, reasoning daily in the school of Tyrannus. And this continued for two years, so that all who dwelt in Asia heard the word of the Lord Jesus, both Jews and Greeks. – Acts 19:8-10*

Paul's gospel was the gospel of Jesus Christ; not the gospel of the resurrection or the gospel of you-must-be-born-again! These are critical doctrines of the Kingdom faith, but they are simply the means to an end -- not the end. The resurrection is the gateway to the Kingdom that provides access to a new life in the Spirit of God.

8

The Domination of Satan

Jesus preached a very radical, but consistent message of the Kingdom. His gospel of the Kingdom emphasized that the rule and reign of God had become a reality in the ministry and person of Jesus Christ. Prior to the coming of *Yeshua Hamashiach*, Jesus the Messiah, who was in dominion?

Let's discuss dominion a little bit. The first time we are introduced with the word and concept of dominion is in the book of Genesis:

> *Then God said, "Let Us make man in Our image, according to Our likeness; let them have dominion over the fish of the sea, over the birds of the air, and over the cattle, over all the earth and over every creeping thing that creeps on the earth." So God created man in His own image; in the image of God He created him; male and female He created them. Then God blessed them, and God said to them, "Be fruitful and multiply; fill the earth and subdue it; have dominion over the fish of the sea, over the birds of the air, and over every living thing that moves on the earth." – Genesis 1:26-28*

The Hebrew word for "dominion" is *rahdah*, which means "to dominate, rule and to have dominion." God gave man dominion over the animal kingdom. When man was first created, God subjugated every living creature unto him. Man had no fear whatsoever of animals, lions, or any other fierce animal. Some scholars even believe that there were originally huge animals or dinosaurs in the Garden of Eden. Whatever animals existed during creation that are alive or extinct today were originally subject to Adam. Adam had dominion over the animal kingdom, and it was his responsibility to subjugate and take authority over them.

The Bible states that God gave directives to Adam: to be fruitful and multiply, fill the earth and subdue it, and have dominion (Genesis 1:28). Then, the Bible states that He placed the man in the garden to tend and to keep it (Genesis 2:15), literally "to watch over and be sensitive about it." He also gave man judicial parameters – not to eat of the Tree of the Knowledge of Good and Evil (Genesis 2:17). Then God saw that Adam and the animal kingdom were not socially compatible and declared that it was "not good for man to be alone" (Genesis 2:18). So God created a helpmate for Adam – someone who could provide both social and sexual compatibility. God created a woman from the rib of man (Genesis 2:21-22); woman means "man with a womb." Adam became very attached to this woman, not at the hip, but at the rib, close to his heart.

Satan, who was cast out of heaven for seeking to raise His throne above God, had already been cast down to the earth where man had dominion. Isaiah records this event:

> *"How you are fallen from heaven,*
> *O Lucifer, son of the morning!*
> *How you are cut down to the ground,*
> *You who weakened the nations!*
> *For you have said in your heart:*
> *'I will ascend into heaven,*
> *I will exalt my throne above the stars of God;*
> *I will also sit on the mount of the congregation*
> *On the farthest sides of the north;*
> *I will ascend above the heights of the clouds,*
> *I will be like the Most High.'*
> *Yet you shall be brought down to Sheol,*
> *To the lowest depths of the Pit.*

"Those who see you will gaze at you,
And consider you, saying:
'Is this the man who made the earth tremble,
Who shook Kingdoms,
Who made the world as a wilderness
And destroyed its cities,
Who did not open the house of his prisoners?' – Isaiah 14:12-17

Satan's former name was Lucifer or Daystar; he was one of the ranking angels in the highest class of the angelic hosts, the cherubim. He was considered, by most scholars, an archangel, a honor he shared with Gabriel and Michael. Lucifer was lifted up in pride because of his splendor and his skill sets. Thus, he attempted to lead a rebellion against God, forgetting that his beauty was reflected and that he was simply a created being. He thought he could actually be like God. He said in his heart that he would ascend, exalt, and sit on a throne above God!

Ezekiel also provides insights on Satan as well; however, we must be aware that a real actual king of Tyre existed (Ezekiel 28:11-19). Some scholars take a dual interpretive approach to this text interpreting that the king of Tyre is a type of Satan. However, some of the language and descriptions do not appear to relate to a human being. Let's explore the text. The language that "you were in Eden, the garden of God" seems to be relevant to Satan (v. 13). Then the text lists that every precious stone was his covering. These stones are the exact stones found in the breastplate of the Aaronic priesthood who served as representatives of God, which suggests that there was a great connection between God and Lucifer. Then it states, "You were the anointed cherub," which is an angelic class who were actually on the holy mountain or high place of God. This text, like the Isaiah text, addresses the iniquity or violation of Satan and his expulsion out of heaven. Both texts refer to him being cast down. Even Jesus states in conversation with His disciples that He saw Satan fall in Luke 10:18, "And He said to them, "I saw Satan fall like lightning from heaven."

Satan lost his position of honor and privilege and was appointed to eternal damnation at an appointed time. Until then, God uses him for His purpose.

Moreover the word of the Lord came to me, saying, "Son of man, take up a lamentation for the king of Tyre, and say to him, 'Thus says the Lord God:

"You were the seal of perfection,
Full of wisdom and perfect in beauty.
You were in Eden, the garden of God;
Every precious stone was your covering:
The sardius, topaz, and diamond,
Beryl, onyx, and jasper,
Sapphire, turquoise, and emerald with gold.
The workmanship of your timbrels and pipes
Was prepared for you on the day you were created.
"You were the anointed cherub who covers;
I established you;
You were on the holy mountain of God;
You walked back and forth in the midst of fiery stones.
You were perfect in your ways from the day you were created,
Till iniquity was found in you.
"By the abundance of your trading
You became filled with violence within,
And you sinned;
Therefore I cast you as a profane thing
Out of the mountain of God;
And I destroyed you, O covering cherub,
From the midst of the fiery stones.
"Your heart was lifted up because of your beauty;
You corrupted your wisdom for the sake of your splendor;
I cast you to the ground,
I laid you before kings,
That they might gaze at you. – Ezekiel 28:11-17

After Lucifer's banishment, he was then found in the Garden of Eden embodied in the serpent, which was more cunning by nature than any beast of the field. Satan, whose name means "deceiver," chose to use the most deceptive animal in creation and to approach the woman. Thus, Satan began his strategy to exalt himself above God again – this time in the kingdom given to the humans. Thus, he approached Eve, apparently knowing that the Tree of the Knowledge of Good and Evil was off limits to them. Since he had been in the atmosphere of God, as a former cherub, he was aware of the protocol of God. Violation of the protocol and order of God is what got him thrown out of the atmosphere of God. In the Garden of Eden, he used the animal kingdom to deceive man, disqualify man, and usurp his dominion.

First, Satan pulled Eve into an out-of-bounds conversation, and when he saw that she was willing to listen, he worked on her perception and understanding. He said to her, "Has God indeed said, 'You shall not eat of every tree of the garden'?"

> *Now the serpent was more cunning than any beast of the field which the Lord God had made. And he said to the woman, "Has God indeed said, 'You shall not eat of every tree of the garden'?" – Genesis 3:1*

Through the serpent, Satan immediately caused the woman to doubt Adam's communication to her by asking a doubt-filled question. This is how Satan deceives so many people today who are suppose to have a relationship with God: "Did God really say that in the Bible?" they ask, though God made it clear in His Word. After he got the woman to question whether or not Adam had accurately communicated what God said to them, she saw the tree differently than she had ever before. She no longer saw the danger of the tree, but the potential of the tree. She now saw the tree and its fruit as that which could make her wise and to be like God:

> *And the woman said to the serpent, "We may eat the fruit of the trees of the garden; but of the fruit of the tree which is in the midst of the garden, God has said, 'You shall not eat it, nor shall you touch it, lest you die.' " Then the serpent said to the woman, "You will not surely die. For God knows that in the day you eat of it your eyes will be opened, and you will be like God, knowing good and evil." So when the woman saw that the tree was good for food, that it was pleasant to the eyes, and a tree desirable to make one wise, she took of its fruit and ate. She also gave to her husband with her, and he ate. – Genesis 3:2-6*

Isn't it interesting that Satan used the same approach on man that he used in heaven, which caused him to lose his position in heaven? He got kicked out of heaven, because he desired to be like the Most High God. He deceived the woman into believing that both she and Adam could become like God, even while disobeying God or thinking that God did not really mean what He said.

> *Then the eyes of both of them were opened, and they knew that they were naked; and they sewed fig leaves together and made themselves coverings. – Genesis 3:7*

Adam lost dominion of the garden; that which he should have dominated was used by Satan to persuade Eve to doubt Adam's communication of the will of God. Thus, she was deceived. However, Adam knew exactly what God said, and he allowed Satan through the serpent and the woman to dominate him; so, he lost dominion. God then held a judicial hearing, questioned every party that was involved, and rendered judgment:

> *And they heard the sound of the Lord God walking in the garden in the cool of the day, and Adam and his wife hid themselves from the presence of the Lord God among the trees of the garden. Then the Lord God called to Adam and said to him, "Where are you?" So he said, "I heard Your voice in the garden, and I was afraid because I was naked; and I hid myself." And He said, "Who told you that you were naked? Have you eaten from the tree of which I commanded you that you should not eat?" Then the man said, "The woman whom You gave to be with me, she gave me of the tree, and I ate." And the Lord God said to the woman, "What is this you have done?" The woman said, "The serpent deceived me, and I ate." – Genesis 3:8-13*

In this judicial hearing, God questioned the accused based upon their authority status. Adam was questioned first, then Eve, and then the serpent.

Adam put the blame on God and the woman He gave him. Eve blamed the serpent for her disobedience. The serpent was not given the right to explain; it was just punished. It is believed that before the fall of man, the serpent used to walk upright like humans, but after the judgment, it was made to slither and crawl on its belly. God announced that enmity would be between him and the woman, between his seed and her Seed (Genesis 3:15). God proclaimed that her Seed would bruise his head, and Satan would bruise His heel. This is believed to pertain to Christ and the serpent. Ever since this time, Satan has been associated with the serpent and the Bible refers to him as a serpent. After God's judgment, Adam was stripped of dominion and that dominion was given to Satan.

There are those who teach that we have dominion in the earth; however, this is not true. The Bible never said that we have dominion in the earth realm; it said that we had dominion over the animal kingdom and subsequently we lost that. We are the most fearfully and wonderfully made creatures in all of God's creation:

> *O Lord, our Lord,*
> *How excellent is Your name in all the earth,*
> *Who have set Your glory above the heavens!*
> *Out of the mouth of babes and nursing infants*
> *You have ordained strength,*
> *Because of Your enemies,*
> *That You may silence the enemy and the avenger.*
> *When I consider Your heavens, the work of Your fingers,*
> *The moon and the stars, which You have ordained,*
> *What is man that You are mindful of him,*
> *And the son of man that You visit him?*
> *For You have made him a little lower than the angels,*
> *And You have crowned him with glory and honor.*
> *You have made him to have dominion over the works of Your hands;*
> *You have put all things under his feet,*
> *All sheep and oxen—*
> *Even the beasts of the field,*
> *The birds of the air,*
> *And the fish of the sea*
> *That pass through the paths of the seas. – Psalm 8:1-8*

This psalm is a reflective psalm of the psalter, which caused him to be in awe of the creation of God and man, who was made in His image. Therefore, he understood that man had been given a responsibility over creation to watch over the handiwork of God and be responsible for the planet. He then marvels that God has made man a little lower than the angels and yet crowns him with such honor. The psalter says that God gave us authority over His works and put all things under our feet. However, this psalm does not speak of man as having dominion in totality; he lost that in the garden. We never regained dominion, and most people don't know this. Why? Because of an overlooked verse of scripture that recounts when God released Noah and his family to restart populating the earth after the destruction of the world through a flood.

> *Then God spoke to Noah, saying, "Go out of the ark, you and your wife, and your sons and your sons' wives with you. Bring out with you every living thing of all flesh that is with you: birds and cattle and every creeping thing that creeps on the earth, so that they may abound on the earth, and be fruitful and multiply on the earth."*
> *– Genesis 8:15-17*

The conversation that God had with Noah is different than the one He had with Adam, because it does not include any dominion language. Why? Because man did not have dominion; he lost it to Satan. Thus, Satan is the god of this world (2 Corinthians 4:4), and has blinded the minds of those, "who do not believe, lest the light of the gospel of the glory of Christ, who is the image of God, should shine on them" (2 Corinthians 4:4-5).

Satan is the god of this age. This fact is extremely important as we consider the gospel of the Kingdom. The Kingdom age conflicts with this present age. "Age" in the Greek language is *aión* (αἰών) and refers to "era, a cycle of time" in contrast to "world, something ordered" or *kósmos*.[1] Christ ushered in a Kingdom age within this present age that Satan dominates. This age is the period of time beginning at the fall of man until the Great White Throne of Judgment.

---

1 Zodhiates, S. (2000), *The Complete Word Study Dictionary : New Testament* (electronic ed.), Chattanooga, TN: AMG Publishers.

Then I saw a great white throne and Him who sat on it, from whose face the earth and the heaven fled away. And there was found no place for them. And I saw the dead, small and great, standing before God, and books were opened. And another book was opened, which is the Book of Life. And the dead were judged according to their works, by the things, which were written in the books. The sea gave up the dead who were in it, and Death and Hades delivered up the dead who were in them. And they were judged, each one according to his works. Then Death and Hades were cast into the lake of fire. This is the second death. And anyone not found written in the Book of Life was cast into the lake of fire. Now I saw a new heaven and a new earth, for the first heaven and the first earth had passed away. Also there was no more sea. Then I, John, saw the holy city, New Jerusalem, coming down out of heaven from God, prepared as a bride adorned for her husband. And I heard a loud voice from heaven saying, "Behold, the tabernacle of God is with men, and He will dwell with them, and they shall be His people. God Himself will be with them and be their God. And God will wipe away every tear from their eyes; there shall be no more death, nor sorrow, nor crying. There shall be no more pain, for the former things have passed away." Then He who sat on the throne said, "Behold, I make all things new." And He said to me, "Write, for these words are true and faithful." – Revelation 20:11-21:5

This present age ends when He, who sits on the throne, makes all things new. In order for this to occur, this age must be terminated and the Kingdom age, which was ushered in with Christ, manifests in its fullness. Satan is the god of this age; he has dominion in this age. He secured dominion from Adam and Eve and now dominates every human being through the fallen genetics of Adam. Satan's dominion over Adam impacted every aspect of human life and creation. Paul writes that through one man's sin, all became sinners:

Therefore, just as through one man sin entered the world, and death through sin, and thus death spread to all men, because all sinned... – Romans 5:12

Paul also writes about the current state of creation and how it eagerly awaits the eschaton:

> *For the earnest expectation of the creation eagerly waits for the revealing of the sons of God. For the creation was subjected to futility, not willingly, but because of Him who subjected it in hope; because the creation itself also will be delivered from the bondage of corruption into the glorious liberty of the children of God. For we know that the whole creation groans and labors with birth pangs together until now. – Romans 8:19-22*

This age has been under the influence of Satan since the fall of man. Thus, Paul writes that we all were children of wrath by nature and were influenced by Satan to fulfill the lust of our flesh and mind:

> *And you He made alive, who were dead in trespasses and sins, in which you once walked according to the course of this world, according to the prince of the power of the air, the spirit who now works in the sons of disobedience, among whom also we all once conducted ourselves in the lusts of our flesh, fulfilling the desires of the flesh and of the mind, and were by nature children of wrath, just as the others. – Ephesians 2:1-3*

Paul explains that when we were born in this age, we were born with a propensity towards sin and disobedience by our sinful nature, which existed due to the domination of Satan. All of humanity was subject to the voice and the influence of Satan. In fact, Paul indicates that sin had total dominion over us until Christ ushered in the Kingdom age. In this present age, Satan rules and reigns, and in the age to come, which is the Kingdom of God inaugurated in Christ Jesus, God will totally rule and reign. Jesus brought the presence of the Kingdom to earth and demonstrated its authority and power over evil in this present age.

Satan is a dominator! He is a friend of no one; he deceives mankind by telling them they can be like God (independently think, reason, and direct oneself) and be free, when in essence, there is no freedom. Either God or Satan dominates you! Satan dominates people on multiple 'plan' levels, what I refer to, for parabolic teaching purposes, as the demonic rewards plan: platinum, gold, silver, and bronze. Platinum is your Satanists; they willingly and knowingly sell their soul to Satan and actively do his will. There is the Gold plan – those who engage in deviant behavior like drugs, gangs, violence, hate groups, etc. Then there is the Silver plan – those who are just self-centered and engage in carnal activities. Then you have Bronze plan; that's the plan for church folks who are around scripture and have learned how to live religiously without Christ.

Satan dominates by blinding the mind, so that people cannot see the glorious light of the gospel (2 Corinthians 4:4). When we are born, Satan has a monopoly over us genetically due to the fallen nature (DNA structure) of Adam; thus, sin reigns over us. Satan uses our own inability to recognize or desire the will of God for our lives to consume and destroy us with our own self-centeredness. But when the Kingdom is embraced, it brings the transforming power of God! The conversion experience provides us with a new Kingdom genetic structure that causes the power of Satan's influence to be broken through the light of the gospel of the Kingdom. Then God begins to reign over us and destroys the power of Satan's dominion. Paul writes:

> *For sin shall not have dominion over you, for you are not under law but under grace. – Romans 6:14*

Satan has dominion over the earth and its inhabitants, and he took it from Adam in the garden. It is important to understand that the sovereignty of God allowed Satan to have this dominion over man and his world; he did not gain the world with power over God. Only God is omnipotent! Though Satan is allowed to rule and reign over unregenerated men, he must still be granted permission for his actions (Job 1:12; 2:6). Satan is not God; thus, he is not sovereign, omnipotent, omniscient, or omnipresent. He rules and reigns as a created being and his power only works among other created beings. God is still in control – knows all and see all; He just operates according to His plan and process of salvation and rulership. Who can comprehend the mind of God? No one. But what we do know is that God has ultimate dominion. He delegated first heaven or natural dominion over the animal kingdom and spiritual life to Adam, then Adam exchanged his delegated dominion to Satan for an opportunity to be like God. Satan now rules and reigns over humanity through the power of sin and causes Adam to act in opposition to the will of God. He blinds him to the will of God, keeps him from the Word of God, and ensures that he does not walk in the ways of God.

Satan despises man in his heart, because man replaced him as a worshiper in the presence of God. It's not personal; he really despises God, so he seeks to destroy whoever gives reverence, honor, and glory to God. God created man in His image – the *imago Dei*. Man reminds him that he was created to be a reflection of God, but instead he wanted to be like God or a copy of God. Every time Satan looks at God's pride and joy in creation (you and me), he hates Him and is bitter about his purpose. Thus, he is committed to cause man to disobey God. Satan tries to inflict pain every opportunity he gets. He tries to cause confusion and chaos in every situation he can through bitterness and unforgiveness. We can see his vehemence by how he deceived Eve and influenced Adam. We can tell what kind of world he likes to create by how he influenced Cain to kill Abel. Satan hates humanity, because God replaced him, His highest worshiper, and gave his assignments to men.

When God created the Levitical priesthood, they were granted access to the presence of God through the Tabernacle. Their assignment was an insult to Satan; their sins were forgiven through sacrifices and that allowed them to enter in the Most Holy Place with the breastplate of righteousness. Compare the covering given to Satan, God's former representative with the priesthood, God's new representatives:

> *You were in Eden, the garden of God;*
> *Every precious stone was your covering:*
> *The sardius, topaz, and diamond, Beryl, onyx, and jasper,*
> *Sapphire, turquoise, and emerald with gold.*
> *The workmanship of your timbrels and pipes*
> *Was prepared for you on the day you were created.*
> *"You were the anointed cherub who covers;*
> *I established you; You were on the holy mountain of God;*
> *You walked back and forth in the midst of fiery stones. – Ezekiel 28:13-14*

You shall make the breastplate of judgment. Artistically woven according to the workmanship of the ephod you shall make it: of gold, blue, purple, and scarlet thread, and fine woven linen, you shall make it. It shall be doubled into a square: a span shall be its length, and a span shall be its width. And you shall put settings of stones in it, four rows of stones: The first row shall be a sardius, a topaz, and an emerald; this shall be the first row; the second row shall be a turquoise, a sapphire, and a diamond; the third row, a jacinth, an agate, and an amethyst; and the fourth row, a beryl, an onyx, and a jasper. They shall be set in gold settings. And the stones shall have the names of the sons of Israel, twelve according to their names, like the engravings of a signet, each one with its own name; they shall be according to the twelve tribes. – Exodus 28:15-21

Notice – the stones that were used as the covering for Satan were now used as the covering for the priesthood. Satan walked in the throne room of God, and now the priest accessed the Most Holy Place. This probably caused a hurricane inside of Satan, who was already full of pride and impressed with his trade. Now to see humans walk in it, he was probably furious. So, the Bible teaches that Satan seeks an opportunity to bring havoc and destruction in man's world (John 10:10). However, he is the god of this world, not the God of the world and must operate according to protocol. He has dominion; thus, he can impact and influence man's world with natural disasters, inflict physical illness, and cause him to murder and self-destruct. The scripture shows us that he seeks opportunity to inflict pain and suffering upon all of God's creation (1 Peter 5:8). Satan is the king of this age, the age of fallen humanity and corrupt creation, who seeks to kill, steal, and destroy:

The thief does not come except to steal, and to kill, and to destroy. – John 10:10

Satan is a thief, who stole dominion from man, and is bent towards destroying him by any means necessary. He utilizes the method of divide and conquer as his main global attack. And he looks for opportunities to inflict sickness and disease based upon the human fallen state. Genetically-related sicknesses and diseases are lawful in this age, because humans have sinful flesh to which they can attach. Because of the fall, humans now must die a physical death. Satan deceived humanity to that state and demonstrated that he had mastery over them through the serpent. Because Satan is the god of this age, he inflicts disease on dying man. But because God maintains sovereignty over the world, Satan can inflict sickness and disease upon a person, but he cannot determine the time of death. Death is based upon the sovereign date of God (Hebrews 9:27). So, God appoints the time of death; Satan chooses the type of death for he has freedom to rule his kingdom, the kingdom of this age.

Satan's vindictive advantages were really launched upon Israel, because they were God's original covenant people, especially loved by Him though despite their disobedience and obstinacy. The Tabernacle was one of the greatest insults to Satan; it was the place where humans received God's forgiveness. You see his hatred for God's chosen people, Israel, nearly throughout their history. The Intertestamental Period, the time between Malachi and Matthew, was a period of great political, social, literary, and doctrinal development for the Jewish people. Included in this period was development and change in the understanding of the Kingdom of God. As mentioned in previous chapters, the prevailing hope of the prophets was the restoration of a historical and political kingdom. However, the apocalyptic writers and Jewish people realized that the world had become so full of Satan's evil that in order for the Kingdom of God to manifest and the Messiah to sit on the throne of David, this present world would have to be done away with. The prophecies of the Kingdom of God became more apocalyptic after the dreadful persecution launched against Israel by Antiochus Epiphanes, the king of Syria from 175-164 BC (also known as "Mad Dog"). With an aim to hellenize them, he attempted to totally wipe out the sacred practices of the Jews and demanded that everyone be subject to Greek culture. His actions, first calling for the massacre of young and old, women and children, virgins and infants in Jerusalem, left 40,000 dead and 40,000 enslaved within a three day period. Afterward, he outlawed all Jewish rites and traditions and ordered them to worship Zeus as the supreme god.[2]

---

2 2 Maccabees 6:1–12

This led to the revolt of the Maccabees, a Jewish national resistance against religious and cultural oppression; the Jews refused to give over to Greek life and religious practices. This terrible persecution and war caused the Jews to conclude that hell on earth was the result of cosmic turmoil. Thus, they believed in the Day of the Lord – a dispensation of restoration, which would involve doing away with evil completely and the overturning of the effects of Satan upon Israel. This is how diligent Satan was in his attack on the Jewish nation to subvert them. Even after the inauguration of the Kingdom, Satan continued to attack Israel through the Holocaust; and since becoming a nation again in 1948 (biblical prophecy that has come true), they are always under threat today.

When the church was invited into the inner chambers of God and could access God through Jesus the Messiah and became His royal priesthood (1 Peter 2:9), Satan launched an all-out attack against the church. This began an era of Christian persecution, through Nero and other Roman emperors or kings through whom Satan ruled and reigned until the 4th century. Then, he launched his master plan against Christianity – the assimilation of the faith into the Roman Empire. Whenever God has chosen a person or vessel, Satan launches a violent attack against them. He did so with the Jewish people and oppression and he did so with Christ through the cross. He did so with the church in persecution; he did so with the church and the faith in Romanization, colonization, and Europeanized Protestantism. These attempts were to maintain his rule among humans and cause them to pay for their violation to God, just as he did. In the book of Job, the true mentality and attitude of Satan towards man and God's creation is demonstrated. We see his desire to inflict pain and kill, cause natural disasters, and divide and conquer.

> *Now there was a day when the sons of God came to present themselves before the Lord, and Satan also came among them. And the Lord said to Satan, "From where do you come?" So Satan answered the Lord and said, "From going to and fro on the earth, and from walking back and forth on it." Then the Lord said to Satan, "Have you considered My servant Job, that there is none like him on the earth, a blameless and upright man, one who fears God and shuns evil?" So Satan answered the Lord and said, "Does*

Job fear God for nothing? Have You not made a hedge around him, around his household, and around all that he has on every side? You have blessed the work of his hands, and his possessions have increased in the land. But now, stretch out Your hand and touch all that he has, and he will surely curse You to Your face!"

And the Lord said to Satan, "Behold, all that he has is in your power; only do not lay a hand on his person." So Satan went out from the presence of the Lord. Now there was a day when his sons and daughters were eating and drinking wine in their oldest brother's house; and a messenger came to Job and said, "The oxen were plowing and the donkeys feeding beside them, when the Sabeans raided them and took them away—indeed they have killed the servants with the edge of the sword; and I alone have escaped to tell you!"

While he was still speaking, another also came and said, "The fire of God fell from heaven and burned up the sheep and the servants, and consumed them; and I alone have escaped to tell you!" While he was still speaking, another also came and said, "The Chaldeans formed three bands, raided the camels and took them away, yes, and killed the servants with the edge of the sword; and I alone have escaped to tell you!" While he was still speaking, another also came and said, "Your sons and daughters were eating and drinking wine in their oldest brother's house, and suddenly a great wind came from across the wilderness and struck the four corners of the house, and it fell on the young people, and they are dead; and I alone have escaped to tell you!" Then Job arose, tore his robe, and shaved his head; and he fell to the ground and worshiped. And he said:

> *"Naked I came from my mother's womb,*
> *And naked shall I return there.*
> *The Lord gave, and the Lord has taken away;*
> *Blessed be the name of the Lord."*

In all this Job did not sin nor charge God with wrong. – Job 1:6-22

Again, there was a day when the sons of God came to present themselves before the Lord, and Satan came also among them to present himself before the Lord. And the Lord said to Satan, "From where do you come?" Satan answered the Lord and said, "From going to and fro on the earth, and from walking back and forth on it." Then the Lord said to Satan, "Have you considered My servant Job, that there is none like him on the earth, a blameless and upright man, one who fears God and shuns evil? And still he holds fast to his integrity, although you incited Me against him, to destroy him without cause." So Satan answered the Lord and said, "Skin for skin! Yes, all that a man has he will give for his life.

But stretch out Your hand now, and touch his bone and his flesh, and he will surely curse You to Your face!" And the Lord said to Satan, "Behold, he is in your hand, but spare his life." So Satan went out from the presence of the Lord, and struck Job with painful boils from the sole of his foot to the crown of his head. And he took for himself a potsherd with which to scrape himself while he sat in the midst of the ashes. Then his wife said to him, "Do you still hold fast to your integrity? Curse God and die!" But he said to her, "You speak as one of the foolish women speaks. Shall we indeed accept good from God, and shall we not accept adversity?" In all this Job did not sin with his lips. – Job 2:1-10

Job is considered the oldest book of the Bible and provides some incredible insights concerning the spirit world and how it operates. We can see that Satan does not have free reign to do whatever he desires. He must submit to the sovereignty and protocol of God. God used Satan to reposition Job; so what Satan meant for evil, God meant for good. We see that Satan is aware of the hedge of protection that God puts around people, and he tries to lower the hedge.

In an effort to stop Job from worshiping God, Satan uses every possible tool against him in the story. Satan influences other humans to kill, steal, and destroy (1:15). We see Satan's power over the weather and natural disasters (1:19). We also see his ability to cause sickness and disease (2:7). As with Job, Satan causes disorder in the home and uses people close to you to try to influence you against God (1:19, 2:9). Lastly, he uses friends to be judgmental (4:8; 5:17). In this story, we see that Satan is committed to causing pain and suffering to those made in the image of God, whose very existence taunts him to no end. Satan is busy trying to identify those whom he can destroy, so the Bible instructs the believer to be conscientious of the attacks of Satan. Peter writes:

> *Be sober, be vigilant; because your adversary the devil walks about like a roaring lion, seeking whom he may devour. Resist him, steadfast in the faith, knowing that the same sufferings are experienced by your brotherhood in the world. But may the God of all grace, who called us to His eternal glory by Christ Jesus, after you have suffered a while, perfect, establish, strengthen, and settle you. – 1 Peter 5:8-10*

Peter postulates that the Kingdom citizen is an enemy to Satan, and he looks for every opportunity to get an advantage over us. The devil uses fear and doubt to cause us to walk outside of the parameters of God. He also uses divide and conquer tactics to pitch believers against one another. Paul emphasizes the fact that Satan uses unforgiveness as a tool or a device to hinder the expansion of the Kingdom and the spiritual growth of the person. A great example of the effectiveness of Satan in creating unforgiveness among the community of faith is located in Paul's letter to the church at Corinth. Paul encourages believers in Corinth to restore the man who was once excommunicated for his incestuous relationship with his stepmother (2 Corinthians 2:5-11). Prior to his restoration, this man was excommunicated and the believers were instructed not to eat or fellowship with him, so that God could deal with him and restore Him.

> *It is actually reported that there is sexual immorality among you, and such sexual immorality as is not even named among the Gentiles—that a man has his father's wife! And you are puffed up, and have not rather mourned, that he who has done this deed might be taken away from among you. For I indeed, as absent in body but present in spirit, have already judged (as though I were present) him who has so done this deed. In the name of our Lord Jesus Christ, when you are gathered together, along with my spirit, with the power of our Lord Jesus Christ, deliver such a one to Satan for the destruction of the flesh, that his spirit may be saved in the day of the Lord Jesus. Your glorying is not good. Do you not know that a little leaven leavens the whole lump? Therefore purge out*

the old leaven, that you may be a new lump, since you truly are unleavened. For indeed Christ, our Passover, was sacrificed for us. Therefore let us keep the feast, not with old leaven, nor with the leaven of malice and wickedness, but with the unleavened bread of sincerity and truth. – 1 Corinthians 5:1-8

After excommunicating this man, later on we are informed that he repented of his sexual immorality and incest, but there were those who did not want to restore him to the fellowship, because of his misconduct. However, Paul writes that they must forgive and restore this man:

But if anyone has caused grief, he has not grieved me, but all of you to some extent—not to be too severe. This punishment which was inflicted by the majority is sufficient for such a man, so that, on the contrary, you ought rather to forgive and comfort him, lest perhaps such a one be swallowed up with too much sorrow. Therefore I urge you to reaffirm your love to him. For to this end I also wrote, that I might put you to the test, whether you are obedient in all things. Now whom you forgive anything, I also forgive. For if indeed I have forgiven anything, I have forgiven that one for your sakes in the presence of Christ, lest Satan should take advantage of us; for we are not ignorant of his devices. – 2 Corinthians 2:5-11

Paul uses Christ the Passover Lamb as the cultural foundation to his readers to understand the necessity of spiritually-minded living. However, you must be familiar with the Jewish context and culture of the feast to decode Paul's message. The pathway to the Kingdom was Passover; the premise of Passover is forgiveness through sacrifice. In order for God to have a relationship with you and me, He must first forgive us of our sins. So, we must forgive people for what they have done to us, toward us, and against us. Forgiveness is a manifestation of the Kingdom; it is the power of the Holy Spirit at work in the lives of Kingdom citizens, causing them to supernaturally release people of their ill doings. Unforgiveness is one of the strongest weapons Satan uses to control and influence people. As ugly as slavery, apartheid, and the holocaust were, God's expectation, for anyone who has become a Kingdom citizen, is forgiveness. Kingdom citizens must forgive their ex-spouses, unfair bosses, and their criminal aggressors. We have the good news of the Kingdom and the works of Christ in Passover, forgiving us of our sins, so that we can see and enter the Kingdom of God. That's good news – that man can once again come under the direct dominion of God, but this time, his sins have already been dealt with – past, present, and future in Christ. Thus, by grace, we have been saved through faith.

Satan is the dominator of this age who must submit to the sovereignty of God, but at this time, has open access to man because he, man, lost dominion. The Bible refers to Satan as having dominion in this age:

> *...whose minds the god of this age has blinded, who do not believe, lest the light of the gospel of the glory of Christ, who is the image of God, should shine on them. – 2 Corinthians 4:4*
>
> *For by Him all things were created that are in heaven and that are on earth, visible and invisible, whether thrones or dominions or principalities or powers. All things were created through Him and for Him. – Colossians 1:16*
>
> *...which He worked in Christ when He raised Him from the dead and seated Him at His right hand in the heavenly places, far above all principality and power and might and dominion, and every name that is named, not only in this age but also in that which is to come. – Ephesians 1:20–21*
> *Put on the whole armor of God, that you may be able to stand against the wiles of the devil. For we do not wrestle against flesh and blood, but against principalities, against powers, against the rulers of the darkness of this age, against spiritual hosts of wickedness in the heavenly places. – Ephesians 6:11-12*
>
> *...above all, taking the shield of faith with which you will be able to quench all the fiery darts of the wicked one. – Ephesians 6:16*

These passages substantiate that Satan operates in spiritual dominion in this age. His dominion has order and structure in the form of principalities, powers, thrones, dominions, rulers of the darkness of this age, and spiritual wickedness in heavenly places. Satan has dominion in this age, and Christ's Kingdom will have dominion in the age to come. His Kingdom became a reality in the Personhood of Christ and created a clash of the kingdoms on earth.

Satan would not be himself if he did not present a non-scriptural teaching about dominion. Some people believe that we have been given dominion over the world, and we will take over the world. There is even a so-called Kingdom teaching that suggests that since God has given us dominion in the earth, He must ask our permission before He makes a decision (they cite Abram and the destruction of Sodom and Gomorrah). This is plain heresy! God does not have to ask our permission for or about anything. He never abandons sovereignty. As mentioned earlier, even the dominion that Satan possesses is not sovereign; he must ask God to complete his own purpose (steal, kill, destroy), as in the case of Job. In this age, Satan has spiritual dominion over man and influences him through his degenerate genes or his fallen flesh. We are born with a propensity to sin and disobey God; this propensity remains even after salvation and leads the saints to walk in carnality.

Fortunately, it is the Jewish belief that one is not responsible for personal sin until you came to the age of accountability. For the Jew, it is the 13th birthday followed by a Bar or Bat Mitzvah. This ceremony defined the youngster as a son or daughter of Torah. Is there a standard age of accountability for children being held responsible for their sinful action? I have not discovered one in scripture. However, it is my belief that God judges each youngster according to their own intellectual ability to recognize right from wrong, God from Satan, flesh from spirit. This natural age, in my opinion, could range from 12-13.

Satan dominates all humans by using his three historical weapons: the lust of the flesh, the lust of the eyes, and the pride of life. These are the three main instruments he uses to control those whose impulses he can influence. He influences carnal appetites through the flesh, sight, and his most deceptive instrument, pride.

> *Do not love the world or the things in the world. If anyone loves the world, the love of the Father is not in him. For all that is in*

the world— the lust of the flesh, the lust of the eyes, and the pride of life—is not of the Father but is of the world. – 1 John 2:15-16

Christ's mission was to deliver us from the power of the evil one, who is the god of this world. Even when He instructed the disciples on how to pray and provided a model, He was conscientious of the power of the god of this age and the disciple's need to implore God's power to deliver them:

And do not lead us into temptation,
But deliver us from the evil one.
For Yours is the kingdom and the power and the glory forever.
Amen. – Matthew 6:13

In the model prayer, Christ teaches that it is the power of the Kingdom that can set the captive free or deliver us from the power of this age. The gospel of the Kingdom was the good news that the Kingdom age had begun in Christ! The Kingdom age, as anticipated from the Intertestamental Period or the time between the testaments, would usher in a time of strong deliverance for Israel by the Messiah. Thus, one of the dominant and most indicative signs of the arrival of the Kingdom is the power to overturn the power of this age. This is what is understood in the Jewish context when John the baptizing one was offended because of the practices and affiliations of Christ. John the baptizing one was somewhat legalistic and lived an ascetic lifestyle in isolation; this was a foundation for his own spiritual identity. Then Christ comes and He appeared to be a social butterfly – attending weddings, hanging with wine bibbers, etc. The actions and the way Jesus practiced His ministry were offensive to John, and caused him to reevaluate the ministry of Jesus. So, he needed a sure sign that Jesus was the Messiah, as he sat waiting in a prison cell. He told his disciple to ask Jesus, "Are You the one or should we look for another?" Jesus told John's disciple to go and tell him of the miracles that were taking place, and "Blessed is he that is not offended by Me." Jesus simply told John's disciples what was happening, for John would understand clearly that Christ had inaugurated the Kingdom of God.

And when John had heard in prison about the works of Christ, he sent two of his disciples and said to Him, "Are You the Coming

One, or do we look for another?" Jesus answered and said to them, "Go and tell John the things which you hear and see: The blind see and the lame walk; the lepers are cleansed and the deaf hear; the dead are raised up and the poor have the gospel preached to them. And blessed is he who is not offended because of Me." As they departed, Jesus began to say to the multitudes concerning John: "What did you go out into the wilderness to see? A reed shaken by the wind? But what did you go out to see? A man clothed in soft garments? Indeed, those who wear soft clothing are in kings' houses. But what did you go out to see? A prophet? Yes, I say to you, and more than a prophet. For this is he of whom it is written: 'Behold, I send My messenger before Your face, Who will prepare Your way before You.' – Matthew 11:2-10

Jesus understood not only the Kingdom, but times and seasons. He understood that John's death was imminent, so He gave him an advanced eulogy. He understood that John's season was up, and his ministry relevance had passed. Thus, he quoted the Older Testament prophets who recorded that a messenger would come and prepare the way for the Messiah (Malachi 3:1). The miraculous works of Christ were an affirmation that the Kingdom age had been inaugurated in Jesus.

Jesus preached and taught the gospel of the Kingdom to liberate people from the power of the oppressor, Satan, who makes a total mockery of men by influencing them to do evil and convincing them that they have a right to choose to act according to their own desires and affection, when he is well aware that the wages of sin is death. He knew what would happen to Adam and Eve and was successful in deceiving Eve and dominating Adam. Still today, he is dominating and deceiving men and women and convincing them that they can be like God and decide between good and evil for themselves. It is just another one of his tactics of domination. Satan desires to see people punished and banished from the eternal presence of God and relegated to hell. It is his agenda to cause people to miss God and suffer eternal consequence. He did it in heaven, deceiving one-third of the angels; he was successful in the garden and deceived Eve; and is still effective today deceiving the world by blinding their minds, so that they cannot see or perceive the glorious light of the gospel.

Satan dominates the world today through philosophy, economics, religion, lust, power, race, greed, and a host of other effective vices he uses to control men and women's actions. The scripture reveals that the goal of the gospel of the Kingdom and the Paschal work of Christ is to liberate people who were dominated by Satan, under the guilt of sin, and walked in total darkness because of ignorance to the light of God.

After Christ revealed Himself to Paul as the Messiah, He then revealed Paul's Kingdom purpose:

> *'I will deliver you from the Jewish people, as well as from the Gentiles, to whom I now send you, to open their eyes, in order to turn them from darkness to light, and from the power of Satan to God, that they may receive forgiveness of sins and an inheritance among those who are sanctified by faith in Me.' – Acts 26:17-18*

On the Damascus road, Paul received the assignment to preach, teach, and manifest the Kingdom of God. In summary, it was to:

- Open the eyes of the Gentiles, whose minds Satan has blinded (2 Corinthians 4:4)
- Turn them from darkness to light (Acrs 26:18b)
- Deliver them from the power of Satan to God that they may receive forgiveness of sins (Acts 26:18c)
- Receive an inheritance among those who are being sanctified by faith in Jesus (Acts 26:18d)

Paul's Kingdom mission was to overturn the power of Satan, or break the dominion of Satan.

It is implied that people cannot see God, because Satan's power has them bound in darkness. The gospel of the Kingdom destroys the works of the enemy:

> *He who sins is of the devil, for the devil has sinned from the beginning. For this purpose the Son of God was manifested, that He might destroy the works of the devil. – 1 John 3:8*

Jesus came to destroy the works of the devil! The word "destroy" in the Greek is *luo* (λύω), which means "to loose; to loosen what is fast, bound, to unbind, untie."[3] Jesus came to loose those who were bound by Satan; those who were dominated by him. The scripture declares that Christ has freed us from the dominion of Satan:

> *He has delivered us from the power of darkness and conveyed us into the Kingdom of the Son of His love, in whom we have redemption through His blood, the forgiveness of sins. – Colossians 1:13-14*

Paul writes, in his epistle to the Colossians, that the ministry of Christ is the manifestation of the Kingdom of God that brings deliverance. The means to the Kingdom is Christ the Passover Lamb.

Paul writes that He delivered us from the power of darkness. There is a power of darkness. Darkness here has an intellectual, spiritual, and moral meaning. Intellectually, it means "lack of knowledge, being ignorant of the knowledge and wisdom of God." Such ignorance leads one to live a sinful life that is displeasing to God, which ends in spiritual death. Christ comes and shines the light or gives the revelation of God. He also sets us free morally from a life of sinful behaviors, and gives us new life in Christ.

> *Christ brought the light of God to this age of darkness, and made known the King's dominion.*

Paul admonishes us to be strong in the Lord and in the power of His strength, because of our spiritual conflict with Satan, who desires to enslave again those whom Christ has set free. Paul states that we are wrestling with Satanic and demonic forces that are trying to regain mastery over our lives – we must constantly and consistently resist the devil!

> *Finally, my brethren, be strong in the Lord and in the power of His might. Put on the whole armor of God, that you may be*

3 Zodhiates, S. (2000), *The Complete Word Study Dictionary : New Testament* (electronic ed.), Chattanooga, TN: AMG Publishers.

able to stand against the wiles of the devil. For we do not wrestle against flesh and blood, but against principalities, against powers, against the rulers of the darkness of this age, against spiritual hosts of wickedness in the heavenly places. Therefore take up the whole armor of God, that you may be able to withstand in the evil day, and having done all, to stand. – Ephesians 6:10-13

Jesus tells us that when an unclean spirit has been cast out of a man, because of Kingdom authority and presence in this age, the unclean spirit still sees the person as his house and constantly and consistently seeks to return with a vengeance:

"When an unclean spirit goes out of a man, he goes through dry places, seeking rest, and finds none. Then he says, 'I will return to my house from which I came.' And when he comes, he finds it empty, swept, and put in order. Then he goes and takes with him seven other spirits more wicked than himself, and they enter and dwell there; and the last state of that man is worse than the first. So shall it also be with this wicked generation." – Matthew 12:43-45

Jesus revealed what happens in the spirit realm, and we, as believers, must be careful to guard the deposit of God in our lives for the devil is resilient and relentless, and desires to regain dominion over you. But God's Word is true: resist the devil and he will flee!

Therefore submit to God. Resist the devil and he will flee from you. Draw near to God and He will draw near to you. – James 4:7-8a

9

The Dominion of God

We have discussed the dominion of Satan in detail, but now we must discuss the dominion of God. The idea of "Kingdom of God" suggests the rule and the reign of God. Kingdom is the King's dominion! Dominion over what? It is the King's dominion over all the world, Satan, sin, death, and the grave. But it is also dominion over the King's subjects or citizens, who are the domain where the King rules, not in oppression, but in liberation. The devil is an oppressor, and Jesus is a liberator!

> *...how God anointed Jesus of Nazareth with the Holy Spirit and with power, who went about doing good and healing all who were oppressed by the devil, for God was with Him. And we are witnesses of all things which He did both in the land of the Jews and in Jerusalem, whom they killed by hanging on a tree. Him God raised up on the third day, and showed Him openly, not to all the people, but to witnesses chosen before by God, even to us who ate and drank with Him after He arose from the dead. And He commanded us to preach to the people, and to testify that it is He who was ordained by God to be Judge of the living and the dead. To Him all the prophets witness that, through His name, whoever believes in Him will receive remission of sins." – Acts 10:38-43*

The text states that God anointed Jesus. Remember in the Older Testament – there were only two offices that were anointed – the king and the priest.

Christ was anointed as the Messiah and King of the Kingdom of God. The text describes the realized expectations of the king anticipated in the age to come; He went about doing good, healing all who were oppressed by the devil! The scriptures declared in the book of Genesis that the Messiah, the Seed of the woman, would bruise the head of the serpent, and that there would be hostility between the serpent and the woman (Genesis 3:15). God declared that the Seed of the woman would one day regain dominion over the serpent. Thus, when Christ was raised from the dead, He regained dominion and declared that now all authority, both in heaven and in earth, had been given to Him (Matthew 28:18). What was a future hope of the Jews, prophesied in the Hebrew scriptures, became a present reality in Jesus Christ.

The scriptures do not declare that we have dominion; the Bible always states "to God be dominion…" We have to be very careful, because sincere men and women approach the scriptures without the ability to do exegesis or a critical examination of scripture considering the context, content, and the language, etc. This lack of understanding will, without fail, end in erroneous interpretation. The Bible states that dominion belongs to God in the age to come, and that in this age, Satan has dominion over those who are bound by his power. Paul writes and attributes everlasting power, glory, and majesty to Christ the potentate, the King of kings and Lord of lords. He also establishes the Second Coming of Christ and the fulfillment of the last feasts of Israel, the third journey feasts, Tabernacles and Trumpets. Once again, we must always remember that there is always a context for each epistle. An epistle is a letter; in the Bible, some are general and some are specific, but they are always written to specific readers with a background and context that is obvious to the reader, but not to us reading it almost 2,000 years later in a different context.

> *…that you keep this commandment without spot, blameless until our Lord Jesus Christ's appearing, which He will manifest in His own time, He who is the blessed and only Potentate, the King of kings and Lord of lords, who alone has immortality, dwelling in unapproachable light, whom no man has seen or can see, to whom be honor and everlasting power. Amen. – 1 Timothy 6:14-16*

Now to Him who is able to keep you from stumbling,
And to present you faultless
Before the presence of His glory with exceeding joy,
To God our Savior,
Who alone is wise,
Be glory and majesty,
Dominion and power,
Both now and forever. Amen. – Jude 24-25

Peter also ascribes dominion to Christ. He, as God, has dominion over all creation and is sovereign in His acts. While Satan has dominion in this age over those that do not know Christ, Christ has dominion over the Kingdom people who allow God to reign in their hearts, submit to His will, and take authority over satanic powers. Dominion belongs to Christ, because He conquered sin, death, and the grave!

If anyone speaks, let him speak as the oracles of God. If anyone ministers, let him do it as with the ability which God supplies, that in all things God may be glorified through Jesus Christ, to whom belong the glory and the dominion forever and ever. Amen. – 1 Peter 4:11

But may the God of all grace, who called us to His eternal glory by Christ Jesus, after you have suffered a while, perfect, establish, strengthen, and settle you. To Him be the glory and the dominion forever and ever. Amen. – 1 Peter 5:10-11

John is referred to as the beloved disciple of Christ. He also writes and ascribes glory and dominion forever and ever to Christ. John acknowledges both the royal and redemptive work of Christ. He indicates that Christ is the Lamb, great High Priest and King, who has made us a kingdom and priests:

To Him who loved us and washed us from our sins in His own blood, and has made us kings and priests to His God and Father, to Him be glory and dominion forever and ever. Amen. – Revelation 1:5b-6

The church is the spiritual Israel, even though God still has a plan for natural Israel. John makes reference to the Mount Sinai prophecy and declares that God has created this Kingdom people in Christ Jesus. Peter, referring to this same text in Exodus, designates God's new Kingdom creation a royal priesthood. This revelation is reflective of Christ's new creation constituted by Gentile and Jew:

> *'Now therefore, if you will indeed obey My voice and keep My covenant, then you shall be a special treasure to Me above all people; for all the earth is Mine. And you shall be to Me a kingdom of priests and a holy nation.' These are the words which you shall speak to the children of Israel." – Exodus 19:5-6*

> *But you are a chosen generation, a royal priesthood, a holy nation, His own special people, that you may proclaim the praises of Him who called you out of darkness into His marvelous light; who once were not a people but are now the people of God, who had not obtained mercy but now have obtained mercy. – 1 Peter 2:9-10*

Peter states that God has created a chosen generation who has a royal mandate to bring people into the Kingdom. These people will proclaim the praises of the King who delivered them from the power of this age and darkness into the Kingdom age under the dominion of God the King.

The gospel of the Kingdom is about the good news of the reign of God ushering in a new age and dispensation of power and authority in the Person of Jesus Christ, who is both Lord and Savior. He preached the gospel of the Kingdom or the age of God's dominion. Thus, the gospel of the Kingdom is proclaimed and explained in the message of Christ. It is demonstrated in the ministry of Christ as He healed the sick and raised the dead – manifestations of the Kingdom. Jesus was dually anointed – as a king and a priest. Thus, His mandate involved inaugurating the Kingdom and seeking and saving those who are lost. The gospel of the Kingdom tells us that the Kingdom is accessible through the death, burial, and bodily resurrection of Christ Jesus. The cross and the resurrection make the gospel of the Kingdom relevant only to those who hear and believe Him. John the revelator writes:

And every creature which is in heaven and on the earth and under the earth and such as are in the sea, and all that are in them, I heard saying:

"Blessing and honor and glory and power
Be to Him who sits on the throne,
And to the Lamb, forever and ever!" – Revelation 5:13

In this writing, John highlights both the throne and the Lamb; Christ – Lord and Savior. He sits and reigns on the throne, and He died and saves as the Lamb. He then presents the sacrifice as the great High Priest! Praise the Lord! That's good news!

As powerful as that news is, the gospel of the Kingdom, in our contemporary context, has become the gospel of the church. We have totally ignored the gospel of the Kingdom by neglecting its authentic Jewish context and have passed on church tradition that reflects one's experiences and exposure. We have focused upon the saving acts of Christ, ignoring His (the Kingdom's) demands upon us. The fulfillment of Passover was the means into the Kingdom, not the goal.

The church today shouts and screams about the cross and the resurrection. That would be all right if it were followed by Kingdom living. The cross and the resurrection is not the end – it is the beginning of a new life in the Kingdom. The resurrection authenticated the Messiahship of Christ and fulfilled the Feast of Passover. When John the baptizing one saw Christ from afar off, he stated, "Behold the Lamb of God who takes away the sins of the world"! Christ was the Lamb of God who took away the sins of the world once and for all for everyone that believed upon His name. As mentioned earlier, important as they are to Christian faith, Jesus did not preach the cross and resurrection; He preached the gospel of the Kingdom, the cross opening the door into the Kingdom and the resurrection declaring Christ as King.

Christ's life mission was fulfilling the Feast of Passover, Unleavened Bread, and Firstfruits as prophesied in scripture, and inaugurating the Kingdom. He did that as the Passover Lamb, who was tried and found without fault by Pilate, proving Him to be an acceptable sacrifice for man's sin, and the resurrected Lord with power to put down God's enemies and establish His eternal throne. However, Jesus was also the great High Priest in fulfillment of Yom Kippur. In observance of Yom Kippur (the Jewish Day of Atonement), the people brought a bull, as well as two goats to atone for the collective sin of the nation of Israel. The bull represented the sacrifice for sins for the High Priest; one goat represented the goat for the LORD, and the other goat for the sins of the people of Israel. The High Priest would lay hands on the first goat and transfer the sins of the entire people of Israel onto it and sacrifice it to God as a sin offering. Then the latter goat was set free in the wilderness (scapegoat). Thus, Jesus, as the great High Priest, took away the sins of the world, not with the blood of animals, but with His own blood. He entered the Most Holy Place for the last time and atoned for the sins of all mankind:

> *But Christ came as High Priest of the good things to come, with the greater and more perfect tabernacle not made with hands, that is, not of this creation. Not with the blood of goats and calves, but with His own blood He entered the Most Holy Place once for all, having obtained eternal redemption. – Hebrews 9:11-12*

Christ fulfilled every natural religious practice of the Jews that symbolized redemption, sacrifice, and justification. He presented His own blood as the Great High Priest for Yom Kippur and shed His blood as the sacrifice of sin for all mankind. It was through the fulfillment of the first three feasts of Israel that our redemption was wrought, and we now have access to the Kingdom through Jesus – the Way. The fulfillment of these three feasts of Israel was designed by God to provide access to the Kingdom, but they are not the Kingdom. Jesus is the Door, the Way, and the Shepherd who grants us access to the Kingdom.

The advent or the incarnation of Christ and the event of the resurrection were not intended to be the endpoint of spiritual experience; they were designed to be qualifiers for access into the Kingdom living. Unfortunately, the end goal of the modern Christian is initial salvation. God never intended believers to rest their laurels on the advent and the event of the resurrection. Jesus wants to be Lord of your life; and if He cannot be Lord, He will not be Savior. Lord and Savior is a two-sided coin; you can't have one without the other. The Savior aspect of Christ was designed to allow you to have access to the Lordship of Christ. The resurrection was your ladder of escape from this age and into the Kingdom age. Christ's resurrection affirmed His Messiahship; but His Kingship means He reigns in the life of His citizens.

Christ came preaching the age of the King's dominion, not simply over Satan, sin, death, and the grave, but in the life of the Kingdom citizen to do His will. It has been conjectured that a walk with God is a partnership, but God does not want to be your partner or friend. He wants to be your Lord! I know that many of you instantly thought of the song, "I am a friend of God." Even Jesus called the disciples friends – this is true; and Abraham was the friend of God. However, it is one thing for you to call Him friend, and it is another thing for God to call you friend. It is honorable when the King refers to you as a friend; it simply means that He can trust you. Can God trust you? The question you should be asking now is, "Trust me with what?" The clarifying question is, "Can He trust you with His life? Will you live for Him since He died for you?"

Jesus is a King, and as the King, He rules and reigns! When Jesus preached and taught about the Kingdom, He taught about the arrival of the Kingdom of God. A kingdom must have the following: a king, a kingdom or geography, subjects or citizens, government, principles, practices, and a military.

Component #1 of a Kingdom: The King

Jesus is the King of the Kingdom. The Bible states that He is sitting on His throne:

> *Then Pilate asked Him, "Are You the King of the Jews?" He answered and said to him, "It is as you say." – Mark 15:2*

> *...looking unto Jesus, the author and finisher of our faith, who for the joy that was set before Him endured the cross, despising the*

shame, and has sat down at the right hand of the throne of God. – Hebrews 12:2

If then you were raised with Christ, seek those things which are above, where Christ is, sitting at the right hand of God. – Colossians 3:1
John, to the seven churches which are in Asia: Grace to you and peace from Him who is and who was and who is to come, and from the seven Spirits who are before His throne, and from Jesus Christ, the faithful witness, the firstborn from the dead, and the ruler over the kings of the earth. – Revelation 1:4-5

To him who overcomes I will grant to sit with Me on My throne, as I also overcame and sat down with My Father on His throne. – Revelation 3:21

Other passages substantiate the Lordship of Christ. He has a Kingdom that is not of this world.

Jesus answered, "My Kingdom is not of this world. If My Kingdom were of this world, My servants would fight, so that I should not be delivered to the Jews; but now My Kingdom is not from here." Pilate therefore said to Him, "Are You a king then?" Jesus answered, "You say rightly that I am a king. For this cause I was born, and for this cause I have come into the world, that I should bear witness to the truth. Everyone who is of the truth hears My voice." – John 18:36-37

Component #2 of a Kingdom: The Kingdom or Geography

Jesus has a Kingdom, but where is the Kingdom? Some people explain the Kingdom as an end time reality or eschatological hope. Commonly referred to as "futurist eschatology," this approach understands the Kingdom as the imminent presence of the future reign of God expected in the lifetime of Jesus. The Kingdom was expected to come in Jesus' ministry impacting the world by the powers of the world to come in a series of unprecedented and unrepeatable events. This futurist look at the Kingdom does not align itself with the Jewish understanding of the Kingdom, in which God is King now and reigns among His people who embrace His authority and experience His power. Dr. Brad Young states that the Kingdom can be seen in the miracles of God from the Bible, and it is repeatable in the lives of His people.[1] Jesus states:

> *From that time Jesus began to preach and to say, "Repent, for the Kingdom of heaven is at hand." – Matthew 4:17*

In the Greek language, this sentence literally means that the Kingdom is near and God is taking over as King!

> *But if I cast out demons by the Spirit of God, surely the Kingdom of God has come upon you. – Matthew 12:28*

> *Now when He was asked by the Pharisees when the kingdom of God would come, He answered them and said, "The kingdom of God does not come with observation; "nor will they say, 'See here!' or 'See there!' For indeed, the kingdom of God is within you." – Luke 17:20-21*

Jesus taught that the Kingdom is a present reality and that God is presently acting on people's behalf, delivering them from sin and the power of Satan, and bringing them into the blessings of the new, inaugurated order of the Kingdom. "In you" (Luke 17:21) should be translated "in your midst" or "among you," and means that Jesus embodied and demonstrated the Kingdom in His Person. He was King who was establishing a Kingdom.

While the reign and rule of God is now in Christ in the hearts of people who submit themselves to the will of God, there still remains an eschatological aspect of the geographical location of the Kingdom. The scripture speaks of Christ coming in His Kingdom, and the Kingdom as a material location. But the Kingdom geography is primarily God ruling through the hearts of men and women submitted to His royal rule. The Kingdom is manifested anytime you see the power of God dominate the powers of this age through healings, miracles, expulsions, etc.

---

1 Carson, Dana, (2012). *The Kingdom, the Church, and You*, Alvin, TX: Dana Carson Kingdom Ministries, p.34.

Component #3 of a Kingdom: Subjects

Every kingdom has citizens, and every citizen must have proof of citizenship so that they can enjoy the rights and privileges of the kingdom as they subject themselves to the laws that govern the kingdom. Likewise, we must have a birth certificate as proof of citizenship. The new birth is required for Kingdom citizenship. The new birth is the result of Christ as Passover, Unleavened Bread, and Firstfruits. Christ's fulfillment of these Jewish feasts qualified us to live, work, and enjoy the benefits of Kingdom of God.

> *Jesus answered and said to him, "Most assuredly, I say to you, unless one is born again, he cannot see the Kingdom of God." Nicodemus said to Him, "How can a man be born when he is old? Can he enter a second time into his mother's womb and be born?" Jesus answered, "Most assuredly, I say to you, unless one is born of water and the Spirit, he cannot enter the Kingdom of God. That which is born of the flesh is flesh, and that which is born of the Spirit is spirit. Do not marvel that I said to you, 'You must be born again.' – John 3:3-7*

> *Therefore, if anyone is in Christ, he is a new creation; old things have passed away; behold, all things have become new. – 2 Corinthians 5:17*

> *For in Christ Jesus neither circumcision nor uncircumcision avails anything, but a new creation. – Galatians 6:15*

> *...by which have been given to us exceedingly great and precious promises, that through these you may be partakers of the divine nature, having escaped the corruption that is in the world through lust. – 2 Peter 1:4*

> *...having been born again, not of corruptible seed but incorruptible, through the word of God which lives and abides forever... – 1 Peter 1:23*

> *...as newborn babes, desire the pure milk of the word, that you may grow thereby... – 1 Peter 2:2*

As subjects or citizens of the Kingdom, we must submit ourselves to the sovereign rule and reign of God, that is, the exercise of His kingly power. Citizens cannot call themselves as such if they cannot provide proof of citizenship or never follow the rules. Kingdom citizens must come under Christ's rule and accept Him as King over their lives. Only then has one entered the Kingdom.

Component #4 of a Kingdom: Government

Every kingdom has a government; it has a way in which it governs its subjects and promotes and enforces its values and principles. The government of God is seen when Christ handpicked His cabinet to govern and train His citizens for Kingdom citizenship (the fivefold gifts in Ephesians 4:11). No other model exists to adequately describe how God governs His people. However, we do know that the historical Romanized roots of the church did not follow this model. Dr. Trevor Grizzle states, "The Kingdom cannot be understood under the British monarchy and its empire building."[2]

The Kingdom of God is based upon order and structure; and no finer example exists regarding order other than Jesus Himself. Jesus followed orders; He only did what He saw the Father doing, and only said what He heard the Father say (John 5:19). He stated that He was here to do the business of His Father (John 9:4). Jesus was extremely apostolic, which is Kingdom protocol. The Kingdom is governed by Kingdom principles, policies, and polity, which originate from the Kingdom teachings of Christ and are supported through scripture. Many of these principles were present in the Kingdom parables of Jesus. The Kingdom is governed by the hierarchy of God. God chooses His own people to represent Him on earth and to work with His Kingdom. The church is a significant instrument of the Kingdom; it is the embassy of the Kingdom that represents the Kingdom on foreign soil. The church is staffed with ambassadors and ministers who have been given delegated authority to govern the subjects of God according to His Kingdom principles and practices. The following are a few references:

---

2 Carson. Dana. (2012), *The Kingdom, the Curch, and You*, Alvin, TX: Dana Carson Kingdom Ministries, pg.41.

And He Himself gave some to be apostles, some prophets, some evangelists, and some pastors and teachers, for the equipping of the saints for the work of ministry, for the edifying of the body of Christ, till we all come to the unity of the faith and of the knowledge of the Son of God, to a perfect man, to the measure of the stature of the fullness of Christ; that we should no longer be children, tossed to and fro and carried about with every wind of doctrine, by the trickery of men, in the cunning craftiness of deceitful plotting, but, speaking the truth in love, may grow up in all things into Him who is the head—Christ— from whom the whole body, joined and knit together by what every joint supplies, according to the effective working by which every part does its share, causes growth of the body for the edifying of itself in love. – Ephesians 4:11-16

And we urge you, brethren, to recognize those who labor among you, and are over you in the Lord and admonish you, and to esteem them very highly in love for their work's sake. Be at peace among yourselves. – 1 Thessalonians 5:12-13
Let the elders who rule well be counted worthy of double honor, especially those who labor in the word and doctrine. For the Scripture says, "You shall not muzzle an ox while it treads out the grain," and, "The laborer is worthy of his wages." Do not receive an accusation against an elder except from two or three witnesses. Those who are sinning rebuke in the presence of all, that the rest also may fear. – 1 Timothy 5:17-20

Obey those who rule over you, and be submissive, for they watch out for your souls, as those who must give account. Let them do so with joy and not with grief, for that would be unprofitable for you. – Hebrews 13:17

And I will give you shepherds according to My heart, who will feed you with knowledge and understanding. – Jeremiah 3:15

Kingdom government involves delegated authority. God establishes set leadership in His theocratic Kingdom. Unfortunately, you will hear some mainline leaders speaking against apostolic order and spiritual authority, calling it fascist or dictatorial. Many of these leaders have enjoyed the democratic system of the church and the benefits of Romanization, colonization, and Europeanized Protestantism, transplanting the political climate and structure of our contemporary society into church government, rather than modeling apostolic order. However, the Kingdom operates by apostolic government that ensures that the will of God is executed in this realm. Apostolic leadership is responsible for the government of the church/embassy, for expanding the reach of the Kingdom, training leaders, and opening up new ministries. God appointed government in the church:

> *And God has appointed these in the church: first apostles, second prophets, third teachers, after that miracles, then gifts of healing's, helps, administrations, varieties of tongues. Are all apostles? Are all prophets? Are all teachers? Are all workers of miracles? – 1 Corinthians 12:28-29*

The gospel of the Kingdom is not Kingdom disorder with no purpose, but an apostolic Kingdom with a definite assignment; a Kingdom that constantly sends generations of leaders to carry the banner of the Kingdom to the ends of the earth.

Component #5 of a Kingdom: The Principles and Practices

Every kingdom has laws and philosophies that guide the conscience and behavior of its citizens. Every country has a set of prescribed and recommended values that are designed to foster the ethos and identity within its society. The Kingdom citizen must be influenced by the Word of God and the Holy Spirit. One of the roles of the Holy Spirit is reminding the citizen of the teachings of the Messiah (John 14:26). Thus, it is the citizen's responsibility to study the Word of God for it informs us of the expected beliefs and behaviors of the Kingdom citizen.

> *Your word is a lamp to my feet and a light to my path. – Psalm 119:105*

> *Be diligent to present yourself approved to God, a worker who does not need to be ashamed, rightly dividing the word of truth. – 2 Timothy 2:15*

Then Jesus said to those Jews who believed Him, "If you abide in My word, you are My disciples indeed. And you shall know the truth, and the truth shall make you free." – John 8:31-32

...as newborn babes, desire the pure milk of the word, that you may grow thereby, if indeed you have tasted that the Lord is gracious. – 1 Peter 2:2-3

Take heed to yourself and to the doctrine. Continue in them, for in doing this you will save both yourself and those who hear you. – 1 Timothy 4:16

Jesus answered and said to them, "You are mistaken, not knowing the Scriptures nor the power of God. – Matthew 22:29

Without explaining each of these verses, what they have in common is the importance and necessity of the believer consistently studying the Word of God as the guiding principles that provide insight for living and illumination of God's will. Every Kingdom citizen diligently studies the Word of God, not because they are commanded to, but because they need it to understand the will of the King. The Bible states that desire for the Word is one of the clear signs that a person's citizenship of the Kingdom of God is valid.

Component #6 of a Kingdom: The Military

The Bible refers to God as Yahweh Sabbaoth, the "Lord of hosts or the Lord God of an army." God commands an army of angels, as well as militant Kingdom citizens, who are aggressively advancing the Kingdom of God.

In the year that King Uzziah died, I saw the Lord sitting on a throne, high and lifted up, and the train of His robe filled the temple. Above it stood seraphim; each one had six wings: with two he covered his face, with two he covered his feet, and with two he flew. And one cried to another and said:

"Holy, holy, holy is the Lord of hosts;
The whole earth is full of His glory!"

> *And the posts of the door were shaken by the voice of him who cried out, and the house was filled with smoke. So I said:*
>
> *"Woe is me, for I am undone!*
> *Because I am a man of unclean lips,*
> *And I dwell in the midst of a people of unclean lips;*
> *For my eyes have seen the King,*
> *The Lord of hosts." – Isaiah 6:1-5*

This prophetic writer refers to God as a King, who is the Lord of an army; the King who commands cherubim and seraphim. His army of angels and citizens fight and war in this age on behalf of the Kingdom of God. The angels are fighting in the spirit realm for the Kingdom citizens (Hebrews 1:14) based upon the Word of God (ascending and descending upon the Word). Kingdom citizens are warring with authority over the power of demonic principalities and powers, against the rulers of the darkness of this age, against spiritual hosts of wickedness in the heavenly places.

> *Then the seventy returned with joy, saying, "Lord, even the demons are subject to us in Your name." And He said to them, "I saw Satan fall like lightning from heaven. Behold, I give you the authority to trample on serpents and scorpions, and over all the power of the enemy, and nothing shall by any means hurt you. – Luke 10:17-19*
>
> *For though we walk in the flesh, we do not war according to the flesh. For the weapons of our warfare are not carnal but mighty in God for pulling down strongholds, casting down arguments and every high thing that exalts itself against the knowledge of God, bringing every thought into captivity to the obedience of Christ, and being ready to punish all disobedience when your obedience is fulfilled. – 2 Corinthians 10:3-6*

The Kingdom citizen is engaged in spiritual warfare as they advance the reach and message of the Kingdom worldwide. The Bible identifies believers as the Body of Christ, and Jesus is the Head of His body. The good news is that Satan is under the feet of Kingdom citizens. As long as the citizen remains in Christ, they have authority over Satan.

And He put all things under His feet, and gave Him to be head over all things to the church, which is His body, the fullness of Him who fills all in all. – Ephesians 1:22-23

Satan operates in the dominion of oppression through sickness, disease, pain, and suffering while ensuring that people remain in darkness. God operates in the dominion of liberation that sets the captives free. The gospel of the Kingdom is good news to all those who are held captive by the oppressive power of Satan.

Christ came to manifest the Kingdom and render the dominion of Satan inoperable. Thus, Christ begins His assignment with preaching the gospel of the Kingdom and explaining the purpose of the things He proclaimed about the Kingdom. Then Christ began operating in the Kingdom reality. The Kingdom reality is the now-presence of the Kingdom of God on earth; it is the supernatural power of the Kingdom overturning the effects of darkness, sin, and death. The scripture declares that Christ began His ministry dominating the powers of this age:

And Jesus went about all Galilee, teaching in their synagogues, preaching the gospel of the kingdom, and healing all kinds of sickness and all kinds of disease among the people. Then His fame went throughout all Syria; and they brought to Him all sick people who were afflicted with various diseases and torments, and those who were demon-possessed, epileptics, and paralytics; and He healed them. – Matthew 4:23-24

Christ was anointed King of the Kingdom of God to demonstrate the authority and power of His Kingdom:

"The Spirit of the Lord is upon Me,
Because He has anointed Me
To preach the gospel to the poor;
He has sent Me to heal the brokenhearted,
To proclaim liberty to the captives
And recovery of sight to the blind,
To set at liberty those who are oppressed;
To proclaim the acceptable year of the Lord." – Luke 4:18-19

Christ was anointed to preach the gospel of the Kingdom, to dominate the powers of this age, and to usher people into the Kingdom of God. This is good news! To know that Christ died for you and rose on the third day, but still be dominated by the powers of this age is not good news. But the fact that the power of God has been released into your life to be a witness, that's the gospel! You have been empowered by the Holy Spirit to be a dynamic witness of the reality of the Kingdom. The gospel of the Kingdom is the dominating power of God over the powers of this age.

The Kingdom message and the demonstration of its power create a different mentality than church as usual. Most modern Christians define their relationship with God, not by the Kingdom, but by the church. But there is no power in 'church' for liberation, deliverance, and transformation without submission to Kingdom beliefs and values. The majority of contemporary Christians have a social religious connection, where their lives are consumed with what they see, and can or cannot have. But the Kingdom of God is about the domination of Satan by God through the now-presence of the Kingdom; it is the abundant life and the reality of the Kingdom manifesting in you – His living epistles!

In Matthew, the Pharisees tried to discredit Jesus' demonstration of His Messiahship by accusing Jesus of casting out demons by the power of the evil one.

> *Now when the Pharisees heard it they said, "This fellow does not cast out demons except by Beelzebub, the ruler of the demons." But Jesus knew their thoughts, and said to them: "Every kingdom divided against itself is brought to desolation, and every city or house divided against itself will not stand. If Satan casts out Satan, he is divided against himself. How then will his kingdom stand? And if I cast out demons by Beelzebub, by whom do your sons cast them out? Therefore they shall be your judges. – Matthew 12:24-27*

Jesus states that Satan cannot cast out Satan, or his kingdom would come to desolation. Christ acknowledged that this age is the kingdom of Satan and that He (Christ) could not cast out demons as a agent of darkness. Then He raised the issues of the Pharisees who called themselves exorcists, but were very unsuccessful, asking that if He cast out demons in the name of the evil one, then what about those who were among their ranks? Then Jesus made one of the most revelatory statements to understanding the Kingdom:

> *But if I cast out demons by the Spirit of God, surely the kingdom of God has come upon you. Or how can one enter a strong man's house and plunder his goods, unless he first binds the strong man? And then he will plunder his house. – Matthew 12:28-29*

Jesus made it clear that when you see demons expelled, you are witnessing a manifestation of the Kingdom. Luke states, "...if I cast out demons by the finger of God." The gospels confirmed that Jesus' Kingdom power was manifested in demonic expulsion. Whenever you see the power of Satan reversed or overturned, you see a manifestation of the Kingdom. The Kingdom was and is good news for those who expected its arrival and those who were/are oppressed by the devil. Jesus came to take dominion over Satan:

> *For this purpose the Son of God was manifested, that He might destroy the works of the devil. – 1 John 3:8b*

Luke writes:

> *...how God anointed Jesus of Nazareth with the Holy Spirit and with power, who went about doing good and healing all who were oppressed by the devil, for God was with Him. – Acts 10:38*

Jesus totally dominated the powers of this age; principalities, thrones, and dominions were upstaged by the reality of the Kingdom of God in Christ. Christ totally dominated Satan by conquering his strongest powers: sin, death, and the grave. Christ – through the fulfillment of Passover, Unleavened Bread, and Firstfruits – defeated the sting of death and took the victory from the grave, thereby making it possible for us to enter into the

Kingdom through Him. The Bible states, through the writing of the Apostle Paul, that Christ triumphed over Satan!

> *In Him you were also circumcised with the circumcision made without hands, by putting off the body of the sins of the flesh, by the circumcision of Christ, buried with Him in baptism, in which you also were raised with Him through faith in the working of God, who raised Him from the dead. And you, being dead in your trespasses and the uncircumcision of your flesh, He has made alive together with Him, having forgiven you all trespasses, having wiped out the handwriting of requirements that was against us, which was contrary to us. And He has taken it out of the way, having nailed it to the cross. Having disarmed principalities and powers, He made a public spectacle of them, triumphing over them in it. – Colossians 2:11-15*

Thus, the gospel of the Kingdom is the good news that Satan no longer has full rein to control your life and dominate your body, soul, or spirit; you now have a choice.

Paul articulates further in this epistle that through the Passover, Unleavened Bread, and Firstfruits' fulfillment by Christ, the law has been satisfied. As the Lamb of God, He has taken away our sins, and through the Firstfruits, He has made us alive together with Him. Thus, at the cross, all of our sins were wiped away! But as it relates to the Kingdom, He dominated Satan, disarming principalities and powers and making a public mockery of them, at His resurrection. Let's look at this a little closer. The Greek term for "disarm" is *apekduomai* (ἀπεκδύομαι), which is a compound word from *apo*, which means "from" and *ekduo*, which means "strip; to put off, to strip or put off clothes."[3] Literally, Christ stripped Satan naked, which was a custom rooted in ancient Roman culture. In antiquity, when a losing king was conquered, the prevailing king would ride in a chariot in front. The conquered king and those whose lives were spared, were chained and followed naked on foot behind the chariot of the conquering king, as it paraded in front of the people. During this parade, the people shouted and celebrated the conquering king. This custom was referred to as "triumph-

3 Zodhiates, S. (2000), *The Complete Word Study Dictionary: New Testament* (electronic ed.), Chattanooga, TN: AMG Publishers.

ing." The Greek term for "triumphing" is *thriambeuo* (θριαμβεύω), which means "to lead in victory and exultation of conquest; to hold triumphantly or triumph over."[4] Satan must bow to the power of the Kingdom! Since you and I are in Christ and operate in the power of the Kingdom, Satan must also give way to our authority, if we believe it. The Bible states that we can do what Christ did, because He gave us the authority and power to do so.

Consider these passages:

> *Behold, I give you the authority to trample on serpents and scorpions, and over all the power of the enemy, and nothing shall by any means hurt you. – Luke 10:19*

> *"Most assuredly, I say to you, he who believes in Me, the works that I do he will do also; and greater works than these he will do, because I go to My Father. And whatever you ask in My name, that I will do, that the Father may be glorified in the Son. If you ask anything in My name, I will do it. – John 14:12-14*

> *But you shall receive power when the Holy Spirit has come upon you; and you shall be witnesses to Me in Jerusalem, and in all Judea and Samaria, and to the end of the earth." – Acts 1:8*

> *And I will give you the keys of the kingdom of heaven, and whatever you bind on earth will be bound in heaven, and whatever you loose on earth will be loosed in heaven." – Matthew 16:19*

> *"And these signs will follow those who believe: In My name they will cast out demons; they will speak with new tongues; they will take up serpents; and if they drink anything deadly, it will by no means hurt them; they will lay hands on the sick, and they will recover." – Mark 16:17-18*

> *Now in the morning, as they passed by, they saw the fig tree dried up from the roots. And Peter, remembering, said to Him, "Rabbi, look! The fig tree which You cursed has withered away." So Jesus answered and said to them, "Have faith in God. For assuredly, I*

4 Ibid.

> *say to you, whoever says to this mountain, 'Be removed and be cast into the sea,' and does not doubt in his heart, but believes that those things he says will be done, he will have whatever he says. Therefore I say to you, whatever things you ask when you pray, believe that you receive them, and you will have them. – Mark 11:20-24*

When you consider these passages, it is clear that Christ intended for us to exercise His authority over the powers of this age right now, and believe in what we say! We should resist the devil, witness with power, bind and loose demons, trample upon serpents, heal the sick, raise the dead, and let people know the Kingdom has come to them! The devil is being dominated by the King's dominion and must bow to His majesty. That's good news!

This is the good news of the Kingdom. The power of the Kingdom is available for you to do what Jesus did and even greater! Demonstration of the Kingdom of God is not theoretical; it's real and available. It is yet another sign of those who believe – signs and wonders follow believers wherever they go!

10

Is Jesus the Lord of Your Life?

When people decide to believe in the Lord Jesus Christ, only God truly knows their heart. However, once a person declares that Jesus is the Lord, then that person and everyone else can evaluate the integrity of that statement. So a better question would be, what does it mean to make Jesus Lord and Savior? What do you base your relationship with God upon? Is it race, class, denomination, or some other religious mechanism? You just read about the authority of the Kingdom of God over the kingdom of darkness. What is the sign that Jesus is Lord of your life? Does Jesus have the reins of your life? Do you submit to his Lordship?

> *Then the seventy returned with joy, saying, "Lord, even the demons are subject to us in Your name." And He said to them, "I saw Satan fall like lightning from heaven. Behold, I give you the authority to trample on serpents and scorpions, and over all the power of the enemy, and nothing shall by any means hurt you. Nevertheless do not rejoice in this, that the spirits are subject to you, but rather rejoice because your names are written in heaven." – Luke 10:17-20*

Though they had been religious all their lives, the disciples were, however, wowed by the power they exercised, becoming more enthused by that rather than the fact that their names were written in the Lamb's Book of Life. Later in this same verse, Jesus prays to God and calls them "babes." The focus of the Kingdom cannot just be the miraculous, because Jesus clearly shows us that calling Him Lord and preoccupation with the supernatural world can lead one astray:

> *"Not everyone who says to Me, 'Lord, Lord,' shall enter the kingdom of heaven, but he who does the will of My Father in heaven. Many will say to Me in that day, 'Lord, Lord, have we not prophesied in Your name, cast out demons in Your name, and done many wonders in Your name?' And then I will declare to them, 'I never knew you; depart from Me, you who practice lawlessness!' – Matthew 7:21-23*

Thus, in order to get a clear idea of whether we have believed in the Lord Jesus, we must search the scriptures and focus on what the predominant message of the Bible is. If the focus of the Bible is the message of Jesus and His work in the fulfillment of the first journey of Israel, Passover, then we must re-focus upon His original message, which was the gospel of the Kingdom.

> *Then Jesus went about all the cities and villages, teaching in their synagogues, preaching the gospel of the kingdom, and healing every sickness and every disease among the people. But when He saw the multitudes, He was moved with compassion for them, because they were weary and scattered, like sheep having no shepherd. Then He said to His disciples, "The harvest truly is plentiful, but the laborers are few. Therefore pray the Lord of the harvest to send out laborers into His harvest." – Matthew 9:35-38*

Jesus' focus was the gospel of the Kingdom, not the gospel of being born again or the gospel of the resurrection. Don't get me wrong! Being born again is a must; the resurrection is mandatory to salvation. But once a man is saved, he is saved. The resurrection is an event that is supposed to lead to a lifestyle, which is the Kingdom. Jesus' death and resurrection were simply your keys to the Kingdom. God has always wanted you to come under His rule; this is what it means to enter the Kingdom. What type of King would God be if He granted you access to His Kingdom, and that was it? Is that it – salvation alone? Truly, God wants to be both Lord and Savior.

We have discussed throughout the book how Christ's anointing was both King/Messiah and Priest/Lamb of God. However, the church has historically preached a message of salvation that does not coincide with the Jewish context for redemption. We have taken a European perspective to understanding the Bible, and I'm afraid that we might find ourselves on the short end of the stick. By believing in Jesus only as Savior, we simply appreciate what He has done for us in salvation, taking our sins away. But there is so much Kingdom living ahead!

The rule of God or the Kingdom of God is only accessible by way of the cross. You have to identify with Christ on the cross and acknowledge that He died a death you should have died. Death precedes resurrection. Upon dying to yourself and asking God for a new life, He will take over your life. Now you are ready to enter the Kingdom of God; His goal has always been to transfer you from the kingdom of darkness into the Kingdom of God. This involves you coming under the rule of God and subjugating your life to Him. Again let's look at the very familiar passage that we quote for salvation and examine the mind of Paul.

> *...that if you confess with your mouth the Lord Jesus and believe in your heart that God has raised Him from the dead, you will be saved. For with the heart one believes unto righteousness, and with the mouth confession is made unto salvation. – Romans 10:9-10*

Paul declared that our confession must be in the "Lord" Jesus, which means "master, king, sovereign," and then believe in our hearts that God has raised Him from the dead. Here, Paul is arguing the Kingdom and Messiahship of Jesus. You must believe that God has raised Jesus from the dead, which authenticates Him as the Messiah, and qualifies you for new life. Entry into the Kingdom is granted, if you also confess Him as Lord; thus, the confession of "Lord" makes Him your King.

This Sunday, churches all over the world will instruct people in the sinner's prayer and tell the people to "invite Jesus into their hearts." Wait one minute – is this what God said He wanted? Everything I have read and shown you tells us that God does not want to come into your life; He wants you to lose your life and embrace His life. He expects you to give up your life, because it is under the power of Satan and the penalty of sin. You must begin to live totally for Him, if you believe He died totally for you.

Consider these texts:

> *When He had called the people to Himself, with His disciples also, He said to them, "Whoever desires to come after Me, let him deny himself, and take up his cross, and follow Me. For whoever desires to save his life will lose it, but whoever loses his life for My sake and the gospel's will save it. For what will it profit a man if he gains the whole world, and loses his own soul? Or what will a man give in exchange for his soul? For whoever is ashamed of Me and My words in this adulterous and sinful generation, of him the Son of Man also will be ashamed when He comes in the glory of His Father with the holy angels." – Mark 8:34-38*

Christ doesn't want to come into your life; He wants to dominate your life. Our sin dominated His life to the point of death; likewise, His agenda must dominate our lives to the point of death. God desires to be your King and rule your life while reigning in your heart.

> *If then you were raised with Christ, seek those things which are above, where Christ is, sitting at the right hand of God. Set your mind on things above, not on things on the earth. For you died, and your life is hidden with Christ in God. When Christ who is our life appears, then you also will appear with Him in glory. – Colossians 3:1-4*

Christ is our life! Kingdom citizens don't have a life outside of Christ. Because we have exchanged the gospel for spiritual colonization, we have socialized the church into our natural cultures and missed the Kingdom of God. The scripture declares to live is Christ and to die is gain!

> *...according to my earnest expectation and hope that in nothing I shall be ashamed, but with all boldness, as always, so now also Christ will be magnified in my body, whether by life or by death. But if I live on in the flesh, this will mean fruit from my labor; yet what I shall choose I cannot tell. For I am hard-pressed between the two, having a desire to depart and be with Christ, which is far better. Nevertheless to remain in the flesh is more needful for you. – Philippians 1:20-24*

It is clear in scripture that the Kingdom citizen totally lives for God and the expansion of His Kingdom. This was Jesus' last commandment while on earth:

> *Go therefore and make disciples of all the nations, baptizing them in the name of the Father and of the Son and of the Holy Spirit, teaching them to observe all things that I have commanded you; and lo, I am with you always, even to the end of the age." Amen. – Matthew 28:19-20*

> *But you shall receive power when the Holy Spirit has come upon you; and you shall be witnesses to Me in Jerusalem, and in all Judea and Samaria, and to the end of the earth." – Acts 1:8*

God has a Kingdom purpose for every believer with discipleship at its core – not money, businesses, success, or any other desire. His purpose for you is not about you; it involves someone else's deliverance from darkness and their turning from the power of Satan and darkness to the power of God. God wants you to step out of the church mentality and enter into His Kingdom mentality and rule, experience His power, and set the captives free from Jerusalem to the ends of the earth until the end of this age! God desires you to move from Passover to Pentecost. This is what the disciples had to do; they had to move from Christ the Messiah and Lamb to the Feast of Pentecost.

> *And He said to them, "It is not for you to know times or seasons which the Father has put in His own authority. But you shall receive power when the Holy Spirit has come upon you; and you shall be*

witnesses to Me in Jerusalem, and in all Judea and Samaria, and to the end of the earth." – Acts 1:7-8

When the Day of Pentecost had fully come, they were all with one accord in one place. And suddenly there came a sound from heaven, as of a rushing mighty wind, and it filled the whole house where they were sitting. Then there appeared to them divided tongues, as of fire, and one sat upon each of them. – Acts 2:1-3

The Feast of Pentecost or the Feast of Weeks is the spring harvest of Israel that occurred 50 days after Passover. It coincides with the Day of Pentecost, in Acts 2, when the Holy Spirit was poured out on all flesh, the disciples were empowered to become witnesses of the Lord Jesus, and the church was birthed with the addition of 3,000 souls. The Newer Testament church participates in Pentecost by being a dynamic witness of the Kingdom and being empowered to assault the kingdoms of this world.

How do you know when Jesus is Lord of your life? When you witness of the Kingdom of God and use the keys of the Kingdom to usher people from the kingdom of darkness to the Kingdom of light, such that they also submit to the rule and reign of God. Kingdom citizens do Kingdom work. In antiquity, in a kingdom, all property belonged to the king and served a function. Likewise, the Bible states that we have been bought with a price and that our bodies are the temples of the Holy Spirit, which means we belong to God (1 Corinthians 6:20; 3:16). In order to be a Kingdom citizen and enter the rule of God, you must yield yourself to God. The time has run out for 'playing church'; that is, not the 'doing' God talks about in His Word. Singing in choirs, serving on committees, and attending church services are not automatic shoe-in activities to the Kingdom. Remember Matthew 7:21-23? Now consider this:

And this gospel of the Kingdom will be preached in all the world as a witness to all the nations, and then the end will come. – Matthew 24:14

The preaching of the gospel of the Kingdom will usher in the end of this age. Unfortunately, this gospel of the Kingdom has not been preached around the world. Through the process of Romanization, colonization, and Europeanized Protestantism, the gospel of the Kingdom has been uprooted from its Jewish soil and interpreted through a culturally biased prism such that it is totally different than the authentic context of Jesus. From this perspective, the gospel of the Kingdom, the main and enduring message of Christ and the early church, has been reduced to the advent of Christ's virgin birth and the event of His resurrection. We have replaced the message of the Kingdom with the means to the Kingdom. By doing this, we have focused on Christ the Savior not *Yeshua Hamashiach*, Jesus the Messiah who is Savior and King. However, we must now take this gospel of the Kingdom around the world as a witness.

When this gospel of the Kingdom is taken around the world, it will not be a religious perspective or teaching, but it will be the manifestation of the King's dominion in this age. When this gospel of the Kingdom is preached and taught around the world as a witness, the lame will walk, the deaf will hear, the dumb will talk, the blind will see, the poor will have the gospel preached to them, and the dead will rise! Where this gospel of the Kingdom is preached the spirit of racism, classism, sexism, and denominationalism will be broken. Christ's Kingdom message was intended to have a global impact and appeal. Unfortunately, modern Christianity reflects Western culture, rather than a Kingdom global experience. Christ died for the world! While Europe played a significant role in the advancement of Christianity, the Romanized church is not the Kingdom of God.

This is the dispensation of the Kingdom, and we must now evaluate our very cultural-driven interpretations of scripture again, but within their authentic context. Jesus was a Jew; He wrote and thought as a Jew, and He never denounced Judaism. His message of the Kingdom must be examined through the lens of Jewish apocalyptic literature and expectation and the Feasts of Israel to get a better understanding of the message of the Kingdom and *Yeshua Hamashiach*. This gospel of the Kingdom must be preached and taught from the context of Jesus the Jew, while understanding that we no longer know Him after the flesh, for He is Savior and Lord of the world, not simply of the Jewish people. This gospel of the Kingdom calls men and women to submit to the Lordship of Christ and to come under His rule.

The Bible states, "And this gospel of the Kingdom shall be preached in all the world as a witness to all the nations, and then the end shall come." I believe that this is an eschatological message and sign of the transition in this dispensation. You and I are the generation who will take this gospel globally and usher in the final journey of Israel – the Feast of Tabernacles and the coming of the Lord and the Feast of Trumpets.

This is a very critical and pivotal moment in Christianity, and I use the term "Christian" lightly. I understand that this is not the way that the early church defined themselves, though they were first called Christians in Antioch (Acts 11:26). The gospel of the Kingdom needs to be preached in every colonized country, as well as the entire world. We need to preach the gospel of the Kingdom and *Yeshua Hamashiach*, Jesus the Messiah! We must preach a gospel that moves men to live for God, not off God. We must preach a gospel that calls men to lay down their lives, not merely invite Christ into their lives. We must move from the gospel of recital to the gospel of the Kingdom. The gospel of recital focuses the sinner's prayer that begins with belief and not repentance, upon the Christmas cathode, and various Easter speeches. Christians have learned to simply recite what Christ did for us, but we do not engage in living for Him as King.

As we move forward in living and functioning on the King's behalf, we must be even more careful to be sober and watchful concerning the devil. This gospel of the Kingdom does not give us dominion; dominion belongs to God. But we can stand in His authority in the spirit world against the devil, always on guard since we know Satan will masquerades as an angel of light.

> *And no wonder! For Satan himself transforms himself into an angel of light. Therefore it is no great thing if his ministers also transform themselves into ministers of righteousness, whose end will be according to their works. – 2 Corinthians 11:14-15*

We must be careful not to be deceived with heretical messages that talk about 'Going back to Eden', 'Sitting on top of the world,' demanding that God obtain your approval before He moves in this world. While we must embrace and proclaim a Kingdom of God message that acknowledges God's active presence in the world, renewing, restoring, transforming fallen humanity and a creation crippled by sin, we should never subscribe to "dominion theology." Based upon a skewed interpretation of Genesis 1:26, 28, dominion theology adopts and adapts the vision of the Edwardian era of British colonial rule at the dawn of the 20th century, urging Christians to take over every aspect of society or occupy till Jesus comes. It suggests that Christians are called to be social activists and return to the Older Testament law in preparation for the return of Christ. This theology opines that Christ cannot return until the church has achieved a certain level of dominion in the world. Unfortunately, this theology has been embraced by many leading Pentecostal charismatic leaders who promote Christian Reconstructionism. They embrace what is called, "Kingdom Now" theology, which is much different from what I expressed earlier – the Kingdom of God ruling and reigning in the lives of those who acknowledge Him as Lord. The gospel of the Kingdom that Jesus preached expresses the "now" rule of God – God is King now! We are not waiting for the rule of God; He is ruling now in the hearts of men who submit to His will. We must be careful, during this dispensation of Kingdom reformation, to watch for counterfeit movements.

I hope that you have been blessed by the teachings in this book. I believe that we are in the midst of a Kingdom reformation. God is restoring the revelation of the Kingdom to His body as He brings this age to an end. Now is the time to increase our understanding of the gospel and be willing to identify error and correct it.

I hope that I have argued the scriptures persuasively to the point that you understand that the gospel of the Kingdom is the rule and reign of God in this age in the lives of those who are willing to come under His rule. It is not enough to simply acknowledge the death, burial, and resurrection of the Christ. You must see the Kingdom, seek the Kingdom, and step into the Kingdom!

About
Dr. Dana Carson

As a Pastor

Dr. Dana Carson is the Senior Pastor of the Reflections of Christ's Kingdom World Outreach International — a Bible-centered, Spirit-filled, Community-building, Kingdom-minded mega-ministry in Houston, TX. Dr. Carson is one of the nation's foremost Kingdom theologians and down-to-earth pastors whose radical message and raw delivery are known all over the world. R.O.C.K. Sunday morning worship services are unlike anything seen in the Body of Christ – exciting, cutting-edge, extraordinary, and anointed – utilizing all of the tools and technology of our current age to present the timeless message of the gospel of the Kingdom of God!

The R.O.C.K has a profound focus on the spiritual and educational empowerment of children and youth, which birthed from Dr. Carson overcoming the odds of Chicago inner city life as an African American boy. His life inspires the next generation to become Kingdom leaders in government, education, business, church, and family. Dr. Carson's anointing represents a combination of Spirit-filled fire and formal academic training, with a touch of the lessons learned in the ghettos of Chicago. Combining biblical study and scholarship, Dr. Carson is frank and real – people love the way he teaches the practical application of the Word of God on a level that anyone and everyone can understand. Dr. Carson is a Kingdom-driven man on a Kingdom mission, possessing an apostolic calling, profound pastoral insight, and over 35 years of ministry experience.

As an Apostle With a Prophetic Voice

God set Dr. Carson aside to be a significant leader in the Kingdom Reformation Movement. He is world-renowned for his expertise on the Kingdom of God (the Kingdom Voice), emphasizing its Jewish context, and its message of the power of the Holy Spirit, apostolic order, sonship, and service. Holding firmly to the mandate in Matthew 28 that commissions all believers to go and teach all nations, Dr. Carson has identified, equipped, planted, and oversees hundreds of Bible-centered, Spirit-filled, Community-building, Kingdom-minded leaders and churches on four continents – North America, Africa, Europe, and Asia, with the vision of planting R.O.C.K. churches on every inhabitable continent in over 120 countries! An apostle, defined by the Bible, he has established three church campuses in the Houston and Greater Houston area - Broadway, Edgebrook, Alvin, as well as lead the church to purchase and payoff 221 acres just 30 minutes south of downtown Houston. Dr. Carson has also trained leaders in doctrine and planted several R.O.C.K. churches in Virginia, Georgia, Illinois, and Texas, as well as over 100 churches in South Africa, Poland, Liberia, and India. In recognition of his exemplary works in ministry, the 2007 Theologian Awards Production and the Tour of Hope Foundation awarded Dr. Carson with the Five-Fold Ministry Award.

As a Scholar

Dr. Carson, though a high school dropout from Chicago, has earned three doctorates and four master degrees, thus he is one of the top 1% of African American scholars in the U.S. Dr. Carson earned a Doctorate of Ministry from Boston University and also studied The Church and Economic and Community Development at the Harvard Graduate School of Divinity. He also earned a Doctorate of Christian Psychology from Logos Graduate School. In 2004, Dr. Carson completed a Ph.D. in Organizational Leadership from Regent University. He also holds four master's degrees: a Master in Counseling and Guidance (Texas A&M), a Master of Divinity (Austin Presbyterian Theological Seminary/Oral Roberts University), Master of Economic Development and Entrepreneurship (University of Houston), and he was the first full-time clergy to earn a Global Executive MBA from the world-class Fuqua School of Business (Duke University). Dr. Carson received his B.S. in Business Administration from HBCU Wiley United Methodist College where he became a member of Kappa Alpha Psi Fraternity, Inc.

Author, Entrepreneur, and Leadership Expert

Dr. Carson is the Chief Executive Visionary and founder of Dana Carson Kingdom Ministries, Inc. (DCKM), a non-profit ministry organization designed to spread the gospel of the Kingdom while restoring families and communities through programs of empowerment. Through DCKM, Dr. Carson spreads the good news of the Kingdom around the world through preaching, education, and literature. Dr. Dana Carson is a prolific author and writer of biblical study guides and curricula. He has written numerous books in theology, leadership, and church growth. Dr. Carson has authored over 200 books/Kingdom resources that are designed to help transform believers in every aspect of their walk with God. However, DCKM is only one of several companies that have been established to resource and support the expansion of God's Kingdom. Many of his books are used to train leaders and laypeople in the Kingdom Bible University (KBU) and the Kingdom Theological Seminary, of which he is the founder and chancellor. This 21st century transformational leader's organizational expertise impacts business professionals in addition to church leadership. An entrepreneur in his own right, he owns several additional businesses: Carson Consulting Group; IntelliChurchTM Ministry Solutions; and FD's Famous Burgers and Chicago-Style Wings.

Dr. Carson conducts professional leadership seminars to community, church, and business leaders worldwide. He is the chief leadership strategist at the DCKM Leadership Development & Training Corporation, a training company that equips and empowers leaders through state-of-the-art leadership coaching seminars. Also a certified church growth specialist, Dr. Carson advises pastors and ministries how to holistically increase their membership according to God's design — reviving, revitalizing, and redirecting churches toward healthy growth for effective ministry. Dr. Carson also provides leadership training through the Center for Church Growth and Kingdom Empowerment, which assists churches across denominational lines, cultural lines, and generational lines, but is especially dedicated to a very unique market of churches and church leaders – African Americans.

Community-Builder

Dr. Carson's fervor for lifting, developing, and building communities is second to none. Dr. Carson studied the church, economics, and community building during his doctoral studies at Harvard University. Dr. Carson wrote his dissertation on the relationship between African American males between the ages of 14-35 and the independent church at Boston University, the alma mater of the distinguished Martin Luther King Jr. and C. Eric Lincoln. Wherever the Lord plants him, Dr. Carson establishes a vibrant ministry that touches the lives of people – mind, body, and soul. In Houston, the vision of The R.O.C.K. and the ministry of Dr. Dana Carson has always been characterized by community activism, community development, and economic empowerment through life skills training. The R.O.C.K. has provided toys, backpacks, school supplies, face masks, transportation, skills development, food, and hurricane relief to the citizens of the southeast Houston area. Dr. Carson provides mentorship and exposure opportunities through at-risk programs for junior high and high school youth, and a special mentor programs for young males of color including the Carson Male Academy and the Young Prophets and Ministers. For his many efforts, President Barack Obama selected him to receive the President's Lifetime Achievement Award, the most prestigious given to a few Americans in recognition of over 4,000 hours of extraordinary service! In 2016, God gave Dr. Carson perhaps his most significant assignment – the opportunity to acquire a Christian elementary school in Nairobi, Kenya that educates almost 500 disadvantaged and unserved children in the Mukuru Kwa Njenga slum.

Evangelist and Revivalist

Internationally renowned, Dr. Carson ministers extensively through seminars, crusades, social media, and television where his preaching and teaching has been broadcast on TBN, BET, Daystar, the WORD Network, satellite television (the Omega Channel and IMPACT Network) in over 62 countries in Africa and Europe; and primetime TV. His broadcasts on radio (Rainbow FM 90.7 (Johannesburg, SA), Sunny 88.7 FM (Accra,

GH), Radio One 92.1 FM (Houston, TX), and KWWJ Gospel 1360 AM (Houston, TX); and TV (Chicago, Detroit, Ghana, and Houston Media Source – Comcast, AT&T U-verse, TVMax, Sudden Link, and Phonoscope) have and are providing invaluable knowledge and understanding for pastors and laymen worldwide. Dr. Carson has been a guest on the Yolanda Adams Morning Show; the Houston Newsmakers, hosted by Khambrel Marshall; and Sunday Morning Live on the Majic 102.1 Show. He is the innovator for the highly successful Relevant Pulpits and Kingdom Voice Live shows on the YouTube Channel – Apostle Dr. Dana Carson, Facebook, and www.TheROCKWOI.com.

As a Father and Husband

Dr. Carson is a devoted husband to Lady Rachelle Carson, who serves faithfully in ministry with him as Executive Pastor of The R.O.C.K. World Outreach in Houston, Dean of the Kingdom Theological Seminary, and Chief Editor of Dana Carson Kingdom Ministries. He affectionately calls her "*Baruch*." They have been blessed with five children: Dana Carson II, John Anthony Carson, Angel Naomi Carson, Marielle Alli Sanchez, and Devon Jarrod Carson.

Additional Kingdom Books

One True King: Surrendering Our Attitudes at the Altar of Revival
ISBN: 0-9780615387-9-5

The church of the Lord Jesus Christ is facing its finest and final hour – a Revival of unprecedented effectiveness! God is placing the church back into Kingdom alignment that we may experience power and authority like the contemporary world has never seen, as we submit our lives to His Lordship. This book will assist believers in making the Kingdom of God a reality in their lives and move them to the next dispensation of theologial awarness. This book is a must read fo the those who desire to fulfill the will of God in their lives.

The Doors of the Church are Closed
ISBN: 0-97816047794-7-9

The Doors of the Church are Closed is one of the most relevant 21st centrury writings to the church. Statistics suggest that nearly 4,000 churches are closing with only 1,200 to 1,800 opening annualy. Less than 20% of Americans attend church and 97% of churches didn't win one convert last year!

Yet, the church has exchanged its mission of the Kingdom expansion for popularity and wealth. The doors of the church are closed! This book identifies the root causes of the contemporary church's failure and raises some monumental challenges to believers.

Lord Help! I'm Trapped in the Church!

ISBN: 0-9746616-4-3

This book is extremely insightful! Dr. Carson has captured the reality of many contemporary Christians who detect something is wrong with the Christian church, primarily based on their own feelings of hunger and unfulfillment. By teaching what the church should be doing, Christians will finally be able to 'put their finger' on what the church is missing – Jesus!

In this book, Dr. Carson describes how many of the traditions of the church have caused people to put their faith in unfounded teachings, Through the principles you will be able to accurately asses their relationship with God and His church. This book provides biblical tools that will empower Kingdom citizens to resist the devil and experience high levels of Kingdom satisfaction and effectiveness. Dr. Carson has done it again by shining a light and providing ways that will help those who are attempting to transition from spiritual mediocrity to spiritual significance. This is a must read for anyone who desires to experience greater levels of God's presence in this life, regain their Kingdom focus, and ensure their place around the throne!

The Kingdom, the Church, and YOU!
Issuse That Impact the Lives of Every Believer

ISBN: 0-9746616-7-8

This book will revolutionize your thoughts concerning the Kingdom of God and its relationship to the church and how they mutually impact your walk with Jesus Christ. The issues discussed in this book are very seldom discussed in church settings, but greatly impact your walk with Christ and with other believers. Dr. Carson, Dr. Young, and Dr. Grizzle provide insight on the Kingdom of God as scholars who are committed to the practical presentation and understanding of the Kingdom concerning modern cultural and theological issues. Your understanding of the Kingdom, the church and YOU, will never be the same again!

Introducing The Kingdom: Your Basic Guide to Understanding the Kingdom of God
ISBN: 0-9746616-8-6

The phrase "Kingdom of God" has become a recent catch phrase in churches today. Unfortunately, while many people 'say' the Kingdom of God, very few really understand how to practically live as a Kingdom citizen. Many people have been trapped in the church and church traditions, and now are seeking to sincerely understand the Kingdom of God.

Well, *Introducing the Kingdom* will gives you to the basic ethos and practices of Kingdom citizens. Dr. Carson has stepped into the Kingdom in this book! You will learn what it means for God to be the one true King in your life. You will never wonder again whether you are seeking first the Kingdom of God and His righteousness – you will know!

Kingdom Change and Transformation: Embracing a New Future
ISBN: 0-97707389-4-6
Research suggests that change is a very difficult process, and as a result, very few individuals ever change! Unfortunately, life and its design are structured for constant change; everything and everyone is in a constant state of flux, changing either for the best or for the worst. Dr. Carson explains, from a biblical and clinical perspective:

- Why change is needed
- How to practically employ change initiatives
- How to position yourself for greater levels of success

This book will teach you how to achieve the much needed and wanted change that you have earnestly pursued, possibly for years, but have been unable to achieve. This book will revolutionize your thought process as you learn how to think different and become a different Kingdom you!

Let's Get Real! How Total Transparency Can Transform Your Total Life

ISBN: 0-97707389-4-6

In this book you will learn how to be real with God, yourself and others. You will find the keys to removing the mask of doubt and fear which hide the person you were born to be.

On these pages you'll find: – Why you must unlock the secrets of your heart. – How God views the mistakes of your past. – The necessity of being honest with yourself. – What the Word says about self-esteem. – The keys to personal liberation. – How to become free from guilt and shame – and much more.

Incarnational Leadership

ISBN 0-9746616-5-1

Winston Churchill. Napoleon Bonaparte. Martin Luther King, Jr. Lee Iacocca. What do each of these men have in common? On any Google search, these distinguished gentlemen are listed as some of the greatest leaders of all time. Their leadership accomplishments are unparalleled, their exploits unmatched by few, if any, of their peers within their respective generations. Thousands of books have been written about their uncanny abilities to effectuate change in their contexts through their leadership. Further, with technology facilitating the immediate translation of these writings into hundreds of languages, people around the world on every continent study their carefully penned leadership strategies closely, attempting to walk in the footprints of these legends and replicate their successes. However, despite all of the books on the shelf and all of the best efforts to replicate the successes of these leadership legends by would-be leaders worldwide, the vast majority inevitably fall short. How could this be? Why do so many fail when following the blueprint of what should yield inevitable success? Perhaps the answer is in the model.

Made in the USA
Monee, IL
26 July 2024

62623698R00108